D0866718

FREELANCER'S TREASURY OF ARTICLE IDEAS

FREELANCER'S TREASURY OF ARTICLE IDEAS

by

Frank A. Dickson

Preface by Robert Stein, Editor, *Redbook* Magazine

Published by

Channel Press, Inc., Great Neck, New York

FREELANCER'S TREASURY OF ARTICLE IDEAS

Library of Congress Catalog Card Number: 61-17157

PRINTED IN THE UNITED STATES OF AMERICA

TO

RENTHY

and our two sons

MILTON AND HORACE

PREFACE

by Robert Stein, Editor, Redbook *Magazine*

Even the most experienced of professional writers go through occasional periods in which they become convinced that they will never again have a saleable idea for an article. Sooner or later, of course, the ideas start coming again, but only after days or even weeks of frustration.

Why do these periods occur? And what can be done to shorten them?

A writer, particularly one who deals in fact rather than fiction, relies primarily on his own interest in and curiosity about the world around him—which includes everything he has ever seen, read about or heard about. Given this wide choice of materials, it seems impossible that he should ever need or want anyone else's suggestions on what to write about.

But in order to write with confidence and skill on any subject, a writer has to believe that his own way of seeing and expressing what he sees are of unique value to readers. As he goes through inevitable periods of uncertainty—for personal or professional reasons—he finds it hard to believe that his point of view can produce an article of unique value to anyone. As a result, every possible subject seems either too stale, too dull or too inaccessible.

One way writers have found to shorten these periods is to bombard themselves with sources of ideas until one breaks through their apathy. Some writers simply read magazines or newspapers incessantly until some phrase or sentence arouses a spark of interest. Others bring out files of old clippings that have been hoarded for just this purpose. Still others badger their friends mercilessly until a likely subject comes up in conversation. One writer I know even thumbs through telephone directories in search of unusual-sounding organizations whose activities might be the starting point for an article.

Among less-experienced writers, this kind of problem is sure to be even more common. Without a background of past success, a writer is even less likely to feel that what he can find to say about any subject will be of interest to other people.

Yet it is precisely because each writer's way of seeing and reporting is distinctively his own that magazines and newspapers can cover similar subjects again and again without repeating themselves. And it is precisely why a book such as this one will not result in a stream of identical articles from those who read it.

To illustrate what I mean, I wish it were possible to give half a dozen writers a set of identical instructions for an article—to report, let's say, on the largest maternity hospital in the area.

One writer, whose bent is scientific, would come back with a detailed report on the new medical techniques for delivery, and for the care of mothers and infants. Another, whose main concern is with psychology, would write about the use of natural childbirth and the emotional advantages of rooming-in. A third, with a sense of the dramatic, would bring back a narrative of the hospital's fight to preserve the life of a premature baby. A fourth, who sees the humor in every situation, would string together a series of anecdotes of mothers and fathers who barely got to the hospital on time. A fifth writer might bring back an article on the high costs of maternity care. And a sixth could easily devote his entire report to the part that nurses play in caring for new mothers and their infants.

Send a hundred writers—and no two of the resulting articles will be the same. Because no two writers have identical interests, curiosities, enthusiasms or ways of expressing what they see.

The way to use this book profitably, it therefore seems to me, is not to regard it as a series of blueprints for articles, but rather as a series of suggestions to be filtered through each reader's distinctive set of interests and talents as a writer. Some ideas will certainly be rejected entirely as unsuitable; some will have value only as reminders of the general area of interest they suggest. But others—taken in the light of self-knowledge—will provide the starting points for speculation, inquiry and development that can result in articles that have "unique value" to varying groups of readers.

As a result, I am confident that this book will be found on the desks of many writers, both experienced and inexperienced, and that they will find it extremely useful and profitable.

INTRODUCTION

How much difference is there between the lead article in a national magazine and the modest feature in a small-town newspaper?

Not as much as you might think. Give the perceptive editor and the imaginative writer a story that appeared in a weekly newspaper, circulation three thousand, and odds are that they'll find in it the idea for a piece that will intrigue three million readers.

Here, for example, is that kind of unassuming newspaper feature with strong local appeal:

> *Christmas in our town, hour by hour.* You start with one family, when the kids awaken and rush to see what's at the foot of the tree; then to the next family, getting ready to go to church; then to another, preparing for the big family luncheon; and so on, home to home, place to place, to give a touching picture of Christmas in your community.

"In your community" are the words that make it possible for us to develop this one story suggestion in a dozen different ways. If you were to go from house to house in my home town—the city of Anderson, South Carolina—you could gather material of interest to many of the 41,-136 residents *of that community.* But if you were to go to several particular homes in Washington, D. C.—to the home of the Secretary of Defense, and next to the residence of the Secretary of State, and so on—you could write an article of interest commanding the attention of the nation.

Or suppose you were the editor of a house organ published by a vast manufacturing company. Then you and several of your reporters might visit the home of a shop foreman for your company in Altoona, a sales manager in San Francisco, a payroll clerk in Chattanooga, and a member of the board in Pittsburgh. Still, your article would show how Christmas came, "hour by hour," to a given *community*—in this case, A.B.C. Widget Corporation of America.

The key difference, of course, is *impact.* My neighbor is known to a hundred Americans; the Secretary of Defense is known to a hundred million. The personnel of Widget can all be considered interested in the activities of their fellow Widgeteers. When my neighbor adds a porch to his house, the transaction is of interest to his family, a few of his friends, and to the carpenter who did the job. When a balcony is added to the White House, the entire country pays heed.

Our job, as writers or editors or photo-journalists, is to find the greatest impact in the idea for *our particular audience.* You can take our story about Christmas, hour by hour, and you can tell it with words or with photographs; in a newspaper or a magazine; over the radio, on television, or on a movie screen. The people in your story can be the folks next door or screen stars from other lands—the Ginas, Brigittes and Marlenes. But no matter what you do, it's still the same story *idea,* told in different ways for different audiences.

There's an advantage, however, to dealing with ideas at the local level. For one thing, the market is diminishing at the top; the toll of national magazines since World War II has been formidable, while the number of smaller, specialized publications and "outlets" has increased. For another, writers traditionally learn their trade by working their way up, and it's during the early stages that they need every boost they can get. But most important, perhaps, is the fact that at the local level you can most easily isolate what changes a piece from a report to a feature.

When he's working on a small-city daily, a newspaper reporter covers an extensive "beat" every day. He proceeds to the City Hall, to the courthouse, the county jail, the government agencies, the Chamber of Commerce, the hospital, the post office, and the schools. He makes these rounds in the eternal quest for the five W's; who, when, where, what, and why.

Now switch to the feature writer. He follows much the same trail as the reporter, but he concentrates on human interest—on revelations, the story behind achievements, unexpected adventure, surprises of personality, behind-the-scenes insights, oddities. He makes the reader exclaim: "That's something new!" or "This will be of help to me!" Besides delving into the "W's," he spotlights the *how*. And when you combine the "how" and the "W's," you give birth to the magic word in non-fiction writing: WHOW!

The beat of the feature writer who works on a small-city newspaper fans out into the section and covers the state. There he finds, or should find, every variety of story: those that will make the grade not only with the editor at the feature desk, but also with national newspaper syndicates, state and regional magazines and supplements, trade journals, juvenile and religious publications, association periodicals, house organs, the national magazines, book publishers. Indeed, the one major aim of this book is to show you that your own city, section, and state can supply and inspire this endless stream of articles and photo possibilities. You'll soon recognize that all the clichés about diamonds in your own backyard are, for the magazine writer, astoundingly true. You'll learn to dig. You'll learn to find the uncommon in the common.

"I can write—but I can't get ideas." Because of that complaint, *Writer's Digest* inaugurated my column, "An Idea a Day," in its February, 1939, issue; and the column has appeared regularly since. From the thousands of three- and four-line story suggestions that have been printed over the years, three each have been chosen for every day of the year for inclusion in this book. And we've also headed each page with notes about meaningful anniversaries and events. There you'll find, for example, that the Brooklyn Bridge was opened to traffic on May 24, 1883.

Our hunch is that a note of this kind can set you off on a story. What changes have there been in bridge construction since 1883? How does one test the safety and strength of a bridge after it has been standing for decades? Who designs bridges today, and where do designers learn the art? Have gullible people really, as the jokes insist, "bought" the Brooklyn Bridge from New York con men? How many companies are involved in the building of a bridge? What are the housekeeping chores on a bridge—the road repair, rust removal, sanitation problems? Who is involved *today,* in *your* city, state or region, in planning the construction of a major bridge? What authorities must approve those plans? The Army? Federal officials? How many highway commissions? Indeed, we could go on for page after page, asking questions that have all been inspired by that one anniversary note. And from these questions may come a story.

The successful magazine writer combines three abilities. He must be able to tell his story literately; he must find the hook, angle, nail or gimmick that makes his approach new and different; he must tell the story for a particular audience. If you write about bridges for a children's magazine, you emphasize one group of facts; if you write about bridges for a trade or technical publication, you select and stress other material.

A few things remain the same, however. Quotations and anecdotes pump your article full of vitality, building the reader's interest, step by step, through episodes that are definitely linked and that support one another. Every article needs a definite theme or point, with all parts of the story designed to leave the reader with the happy thought that he has realized enjoyment or benefit from the feature.

Six steps spell success in fashioning an article, particularly one written for a regional national magazine:

1. Cram the first part with action.

2. Fill the middle part with narrative or explanation.

3. Use a number of incidents or anecdotes that supply a well-rounded picture and drive home a point.

4. Fill the gaps between them with necessary information.

5. Push the action at full tilt as long as possible. Any descriptive material should be inserted after a highly dramatic moment, in order to whet the desire of the reader to read right through to find out what happens next.

6. Devote the last part, like the first, to action; and end at a peak, without rambling or fizzling out.

DeWitt Wallace, the publisher of *Reader's Digest,* has a three-point formula that he impresses upon his magazine's roving reporters: Command instant attention with a striking statement as the opening; unfold at least two relevant cases, as narratives, that document the theme: and conclude with a punchy paragraph that will "tie the wheat in the sack."

Phil Dessauer, a contributor to many fine magazines, has developed "group storytelling" as a source of anecdotes, and he used this method when he broke into *The Saturday Evening Post*. He corrals two or more persons familiar with the subject of the article, and goads or entices them into recalling incidents that yield anecdotes for his notebook or tape recorder. Speaking of his group technique, Dessauer relates: "Psychologically, I suppose, this is merely taking advantage of a natural tendency of people to entertain each other with stories, but it works splendidly for a writer. One person will tell a tale and somebody else will embroider or expand on it—or think of another. The writer's job is to keep the game going by throwing in a question or a directional push when the pace begins to slow down. Any number can play, but two to four will keep a note-taker busy."

He also stresses: "The point is that if you talk to enough people in researching a story, some of them are going to turn into scouts and help you when you least expect it. If you talk to ten or twelve people on a story, one or two of them will actually become a front man for you and field in material. When your research is limited to three or four interviews, this is less likely to happen."

Helen Doss, a master in magazine article writing, always collects far more illustrations or anecdotes than she can use in her articles. The point is to use only the best. She puts aside the best illustration for the ending and makes the most of the next best for her beginning. Then with her abundance of anecdotes she still has a wide choice to illustrate the body of her article.

The successful magazine writer divides his time between writing and reading. It is up to you to read, to *study* the article market; you're the one who must learn the difference between the story that's suitable for the newspaper's feature page and the piece that is right for the newspaper's weekend supplement. You must get to know the regional publications, the trade journals, the juveniles, the men's group, the shelter magazines. And if you do your studying well, you'll also learn the magazine writer's most profitable trick: adapting the same story for several publications.

The very first item to appear in my first *Writer's Digest* column ran: "Photography is 100 years old this year. A story, with local tie-ups, of its progress since then . . ."

I decided to try that idea myself. A national photography magazine carried my feature about the first traveling photographer in America; a newspaper syndicate distributed another story of mine on the same subject; a daily newspaper in my city featured an article I wrote with a local angle, because the pioneer with the camera was my great-grandfather, John R. Schorb; and not long ago I placed still another feature on my ancestor with the Sunday magazine of a state newspaper.

Countless features offer such opportunities for sales to several markets, none of them conflicting since they have vastly different audiences. The articles must, of course, be slanted differently for each publication; in the case of trade journals, for example, you should present "liftable" ideas; that is, suggestions with which the reader can solve a problem in his trade or increase his sales.

In another column I proposed a feature headed *"Prices, fifty years ago."* A reader went through the files of his local newspaper, and wrote an amusing report on the costs of goods and services in his town at the turn of the century. Then he researched in several particular fields—appliances, furniture, transportation, foods—and sold articles to trade magazines in the appliance, furniture, transportation and food fields. Next he selected the few most surprising and intriguing of all his examples, and wrote a wrap-up feature that he was able to place with a digest-sized magazine. When he wrote to me about all this he said, "Frank—that wasn't just an idea. It's a career!"

Perhaps, for you, this isn't just a book. Let's hope it's a career.

JANUARY 1

Birth of Paul Revere (1735) and Betsy Ross (1752) . . . Flag of "United Colonies" raised by George Washington at Cambridge (1776) . . . Homestead Act goes into effect (1863) . . . Issuance of Emancipation Proclamation (1863) . . . U.S. parcel post system instituted (1913).

What's happened to apprenticeships? Interview oldsters to present a picture of the apprentice system that once dominated the trades. What crafts use this training system now? Does anyone feel that the old system produced better workers?

Let's hold a shower. The myriad types of shower given—engagement, matrimonial, baby linen, silver, appliance, and so on. What are the most popular gifts? Present novel shower ideas gaining popularity today among young women.

Banks—today and yesterday. Using one bank, contrast the austerity of the past with the relaxed, friendly approach so common today. What new services do the banks offer? What neighborly gestures? What surprising overtures by mail, phone, and in advertising?

JANUARY 2

Birth of Nathaniel Bacon (1647) . . . First correspondence school for blind opens (Illinois, 1922) . . . Founding, American Psychological Association (1925).

Old photographs owned by athletic coaches. The pictures they cherish most of all; memories of thrilling moments stirred by the photographs; celebrated teams of bygone years. What has happened to these sports stars of yesteryear?

A visit to a sporting goods factory. Steps in the manufacturing process; unusual materials employed; changes in the items within recent years. Officials or sales representatives of the plant who have been prominent athletes. Slant: The hard toil behind products that enable sports lovers to enjoy themselves.

Music in factories. Recorded music, played over public address systems or "piped" in, steps up production, reduces fatigue, and adds to the happiness of the workers. What types of music are preferred? Learn from the man in charge of music selection whether some music is barred—rock-and-roll or progressive jazz, for instance. (In some factories it has been found too intrusive.)

JANUARY 3

Battle of Princeton (1777) . . . Birth of Lucretia Coppin Mott (1793) and Father Damien, the leper priest (1841) . . . Patent granted to M. C. Stone for drinking straws (1888).

Addresses. What are the correct forms of written address and salutation for clergymen, statesmen, Congressmen, dignitaries, judges, and so on? What are special rules of etiquette when being presented to officials? A government secretary or city "greeter" can supply the answers.

Union organizer. Interview a man whose career is dedicated to organizing unions and increasing their membership. His recollections of the old days of labor-management conflict, contrasted with modern-day collective bargaining and union social-welfare activities.

Campaign buttons. A collection of buttons used in past city, state and national elections—along with banners, novelties, posters, ties, caps. Stories behind the slogans and catchwords.

JANUARY 4

Birth of Isaac Newton (1642), Jacob Grimm (1786), and Louis Braille (1809) . . . Thomas Stevens completes 13,500-mile trip around the world by bicycle (1886) . . . Utah admitted to Union (1896).

Finances after retirement. What the reader should know about Social Security, pension plans, annuities, health insurance, part-time income, special homes for oldsters, and city and state provisions for help to the aged.

Your name is on a list. Show how names get on mailing lists; how lists are exchanged by companies; list-rental activities; "sucker lists"; the science of direct-by-mail selling. Post-office rules and regulations for the consumer's protection. A dealer in lists can answer your questions.

Whence titles of short stories and novels? Build this around an interview with an author. Inspiration from the Bible; how certain Biblical passages, Shakespearean sonnets, other classics of poetry have produced scores of famous titles.

JANUARY 5

Birthday of Stephen Decatur (1779) . . . First cable across Pacific opened to public use, San Francisco to Honolulu (1903) . . . Death, George Washington Carver (1943).

Where do they go in the summer? An anecdotal survey of summer-vacation plans and projects of teachers, students, ice-skating instructors, and others whose work "ends" during the hot spell.

Where do they go in the winter? Plan *now* to do a similar treatment for counselors, life-guards, ice-cream salesmen, gardeners, amusement-park attendants, and others we see primarily during the summer months.

Built-up shoes. You'll get your information from a shoestore operator or a shoemaker specializing in orthopedic shoes. How does the "Elevator Shoe" work? What does it cost? What other problems are helped or concealed by custom shoes? Is the built-up shoe worn mostly by men who "want to be as tall as she is"? Or for professional reasons?

JANUARY 6

Epiphany . . . Marriage of George and Martha Washington (1759) . . . Morse demonstrates telegraph for first time (1838) . . . Birth, Carl Sandburg (1878).

Favorite exercises of athletes . . . and gymnasium teachers, dancers, and coaches. Their hints on how to keep fit. A sampling of exercises for such specific purposes as achieving slimness, to improve posture, as an aid to better breathing, and so on.

Why study certain subjects? Answers supplied by teachers of courses sometimes rejected by high-schoolers and college undergraduates. Their explanation of the intellectual stimulation that can be gained from studying Latin, the classics, philosophy, economics or ancient history.

An outstanding business college. How the institution is training young and mature folks—in full-time and in part-time evening courses—to meet the labor demands of government, industry and business. Special training in use of the new electronic equipment. Does a business college have "school spirit"? How does its first year of schooling compare with the first year at a liberal arts college?

JANUARY 7

First national election (1789) . . . Birth of Millard Fillmore (1800) . . . Commercial phone service, New York to London, begins (1927).

"Boy! Did I blush!" A round-up of embarrassing experiences, using celebrities or ordinary folk in particular categories (i.e., clerks, nurses, delivery men) as the subjects who confess.

"Waste" products that are used. The ways in which business ingeniously finds markets for materials that were once considered garbage. Get your information from heads of industries.

Fairy tales—more or less frightening than TV? A debate between a psychologist and a television executive on the violence shown to youngsters on the television screen—or read in old tales and rhymes.

JANUARY 8

Connecticut enacts first state copyright law (1783) . . . Jackson defeats British at New Orleans (1815).

A family budget. A home economics expert, a banker, and an accountant contribute their ideas on the how's and why's of a family budget. Should the youngsters be in on this family plan?

Science-fiction writer at work. How does he develop his fantastic ideas about the future? Can fiction outdistance today's astonishing science facts? Have any of his imaginative "predictions" come true? What does he *really* think the year 2,000 will bring?

Children of an animal trainer. Do they have their own pets? Do they play with or feed young wild beasts? Do any of them plan to follow in Dad's footsteps? Their view of the most exciting stunt performed by their father in the ring. Their store of knowledge about animals. Slant: the love of the trainer's children for animals, a vital quality in training wild creatures to perform.

JANUARY 9

First successful balloon flight in U.S. (1793) . . . Birth of Carrie Chapman Catt (1859) . . . Civil War beginning marked by firing on supply ship, "Star of the West" (1861).

Homeless men. How they find places to sleep; seeking shelter in jail; experiences of magistrates with vagrants; "soup lines" for the homeless; rehabilitation services available; community efforts and philanthropic work to help these men.

Relax, please! What professional photographers do to help subjects, especially children, lose their shyness and "frozen" appearance.

Setting newspaper type by perforated tape. How the tape is "punched" by operators, and afterward inserted in the linotype machine to produce the type. The speed of the operators.

JANUARY 10

Birth of Ethan Allen (1737) . . . Oil strike in Texas starts boom (1901).

Having trouble sleeping? Here are the favorite remedies for insomnia as supplied by————. (*You* choose your own group of accomplished snoozers!) Play this for gag value by taking candid photographs of nappers in unlikely places: park benches, buses, a pew, at a lecture, on the beach; and obtain *their* prescriptions for cat-naps.

What the Federal Reserve Board means to you. A banker explains how interest rates, mortgage money, personal loans, and business borrowing are ultimately dependent on Board decisions.

Parry-thrust! Profile of a scholastic fencing team. Explanation of different weapons—foil, sabre, epee. Introduction of electrical devices in scoring; unusual number of judges needed otherwise. Why fencing instruction is mandatory for all young actors and actresses.

JANUARY 11

Birth of Alexander Hamilton (1757) . . . Founding of still-active Presbyterian Minister's Fund, first U. S. life insurance company (1759) . . . Birth of Ezra Cornell (1807).

Well-known "Georges." Slant: How the saying, "Let George do it," sums up their service to their community. Chief accomplishments of local, regional, national Georges; Georges who have held numerous offices in civic, religious, and business affairs.

Freckle king. The school boy regarded as the possessor of the most freckles. Has he arrived at an estimate of the number of freckles? His preferences in sports and hobbies. Has he considered the use of freckle-removal preparations? Why?

Checking utility meters. How utility companies check water, light, and gas meters; replacing meters. How they follow up on complaints from customers who challenge the accuracy of their bills. Slant: Take it from the utility industry, the customer is not always right!

JANUARY 12

Birth of John Hancock (1737) . . . First public museum in U.S. opens in Charleston, South Carolina (1773) . . . Birth of Jack London (1876).

The model wife. What's the perfect wife like? Opinions by a number of husbands and bachelors. Have any of them ever seen "the model wife"? Have the gals found it any easier to locate "the model husband"?

Binoculars and other field-glasses. How to understand the numbers and symbols that designate strength. What's the correct field-glass or optical aid for watching sports. Or for use aboard a pleasure craft? Or for bird-watching? Or amateur astronomy?

Fire! A fire department official discusses fire prevention and extinguishing. The right thing for the job. Salt in the kitchen, or something better? Where extinguishers should be placed throughout the home; how to pass through smoke or flame with least possible harm.

JANUARY 13

End of hostilities with Britain (1793) . . . Birth of Horatio Alger (1834) . . . Anthony Faas patents first accordion (1854) . . . Death, penniless, of Stephen Foster (1864).

A visit to a fish hatchery. How the fish are bred and cared for; stocking lakes and streams; provisions for visitors; scientific studies conducted at hatchery.

A license to fly. How a civilian becomes an aviator. Training on the ground and in the air. Time and costs. The steps from piloting a single-engine propeller-craft to the larger planes.

Night-club photography. Experiences of photographers who snap pictures of night-club patrons. Their sure bets: for example, photographs of folks celebrating gala wedding anniversaries. Developing the film and making the prints within a short time.

JANUARY 14

Birth of Albert Schweitzer (1875) . . . Ford's "assembly line" in operation for first time (1914).

Food inspection. How the customer at a restaurant is protected against adulterated or spoiled foods. Regulations governing short-order diner and de luxe dining-room alike. Self-policing by associations of restaurateurs. Qualifications of the inspector.

Scouting for sports talent. How college coaches and professional teams seek promising players. The necessity for quick appraisals and decisions. How the scouts get their leads. Their successes and failures.

Summer jobs for teen-agers. A survey of employment opportunities in your community (city, state, region). Average earnings. Summer positions that can lead to careers. Slant: Although summer is months away, *now* is the time to apply for many vacation-period jobs.

JANUARY 15

Birth of Molière (1622) . . . The donkey as a symbol of the Democratic Party first appears (Harper's Weekly, 1870) . . . Death of pioneer American photographer, Mathew Brady (1896).

Fun with fortune-telling. Various methods used by amateur entertainers who peer into the future—cards, tea-leaves, coffee-grounds, the ouiji board, dreams, palms, handwriting.

The fate of the barber pole. Do many tonsorial emporiums of your city still retain the traditional pole with its bright red and white stripes? The origin of this symbol.

Solving crimes through footprints. Interview the local chief of police or the head of the detective bureau about the force's most interesting cases. How footprints frequently provide as much evidence as fingerprints.

JANUARY 16

Beginning of Prohibition (1920) . . . (First state to ratify 18th Amendment had been Mississippi—on this day, two years previously.)

Cat's whisker to FM. Interview a veteran in radio broadcasting on the progress of the medium—from the crystal set to today's transistor sets, stereophonic FM, and radio messages through space. Pin article to fact that a popular "new" toy is the crystal radio!

Treatment of ill prisoners in your state. The care of invalid and tubercular inmates; treatment of mentally ill prisoners. When are sex criminals released? Should they be? Get controversial quotes.

Going up! How the increasing average height of Americans affects one community—higher desks needed at schools, more leg-room required in theaters, and the "average sizes" in clothing and shoe shops are changing. Who's growing faster—the average boy or girl? And what about the width and girth of adults?

JANUARY 17

Birth of Benjamin Franklin (1706) . . . First baby born in White House (1806) . . . The San Francisco cable-car patented (1887).

Amateur chemists. Build story around one hobbyist —extend to show how amateurs in the basement are a national resource. For example—have any of your subject's ideas interested industry? What innovations have come from home laboratories? Compare today's "chemistry sets" with those of other days.

Checking your checkbook. A bank official explains how to keep your records so that your account always matches that of the bank. No more arguments between hubby and wife!

Big board and little board! Have a stockbroker explain the terminology of the stock market, including such phrases as "spin-off," "wash sales," "proxy," "watered stock," and so on.

JANUARY 18

Birth of Daniel Webster (1782).

Allowances and pin money. What do kids receive from their folks these days in the way of spending money? Average "incomes" by age. Any chores to be done in return for allowances? How is money spent? What do teachers think about the allowance system?

Do you know how much YOU'RE worth? Show the reader how (and why) to estimate his real net worth—i.e., not just cash in bank, but degree of ownership of home, land, furniture, car, appliances, insurance, and so on. Emphasize importance of the home inventory, with case histories from an insurance man on value of this.

The steps in preparing a sermon. Methods employed by local ministers; finding inspiration for a sermon. What sort of sermons require the most preparation? Do most local pastors write out and memorize their sermons? Or speak from notes and outlines? What books and magazines do they use for guidance?

JANUARY 19

Birth of James Watt (1736), Robert E. Lee (1807), Edgar Allan Poe (1809) . . . Patent granted for neon electric sign (1915).

Odd reasons for borrowing money. Anecdotes told by the head of a loan company or a bank's credit division. See pawnbrokers to learn about unusual items pledged. Discuss seasonal factors. Keep alert to unusual facts—for example, growth of credit unions.

A modern Demosthenes. A prominent orator who overcame a speech difficulty. Did he ever—or does he even now—suffer stage fright? What the subject considers the necessary ingredients of effective speeches. His advice, pro or con, on talks beginning with jokes.

"Cowboy and Indians." The games played by youngsters change with the news. Once the "enemy" was a "Hun," then a "Jap," then a "red." (But the young ones always do seem to go back to Redman vs. Paleface!) What other reflections of the times—space ships? "Atomic explosions" in the schoolyard? Recount actual games, conversations, and the accompanying action.

JANUARY 20

St. Agnes Eve . . . Inauguration Day (Franklin Roosevelt first President inaugurated on this day—1937).

Worst problems in a city park. Keeping "wolves" and litterbugs under control. Does vandalism occur in waves? Carving of initials on benches and trees. Lovers who grow too ardent.

Dangers in the garage. A safety expert discusses the many catastrophes that can take place in a garage through carelessness. A checklist for the reader to help prevent fire from spontaneous combustion, infected wounds from cuts from rusting equipment, accidental poisoning of children, asphyxiation through carbon monoxide poisoning, and so on.

Gifts that grow in value. Unusual gift ideas for children: such things as a copy of The New York Times on each birthday (for his birthdate, particularly); stocks; bonds; a piggy-bank each year, with pennies saved during the year by relatives. You'll get more (and better) suggestions from parents and friends.

JANUARY 21

Birthday of "Stonewall" Jackson (1824) . . . Atom-powered submarine, Nautilus, *launched (1954).*

Baby-sitting pools. Profile of the members of a sitting pool, and how they trade baby-watching time for free time. Are "extra credits" earned for post-midnight sitting? Their safety regulations. How to form your own pool.

Antiques? Or modern? Arm two couples with a fictitious sum of money, and—in cooperation with one manufacturer of contemporary furniture, and one dealer in antiques—let them "furnish" their dream homes. Photographs and a record of money "spent" make this an interesting feature.

Restoring old portraits and photographs. A day in a studio that specializes in this exacting work. Methods of restoring old paintings and photographs to their original clarity and colors. How an airbrush is used.

JANUARY 22

Birth of Francis Bacon (1561) and Lord Byron (1788) . . . Founding, National Association of Manufacturers (1895).

Kites in the sky. This isn't just a pastime for youngsters—there are kiting championships, national and international. Interview an authority for hints on flying kites, making your own, new developments and styles.

Could you recognize the ——? Waiter who served you dinner last night? The cab driver who drove you to your office? The elevator operator? A story about the people some people don't recognize unless they see them "on the job."

Lighting. What we know about minimum needs for lighting in the home—proper bulbs for reading lamps, in work areas, near stairways, when the TV is on. New innovations in lighting—bulbs that kill bugs, that last unusually long periods, that use "reflected light." Your information sources are lighting engineers or an interior designer.

JANUARY 23

Dr. Elizabeth Blackwell, first woman physician, graduates from Medical Institution of Geneva, New York (1849).

The cost of a dozen eggs. Show, from start to finish, what goes into the so-many-cents-a-dozen price the consumer pays. The retailer's profit, those of various middlemen, the chicken farmer's. It's fascinating (and distressing!) to see the price climb!

The information clerk at a local bus terminal. How many questions does he answer daily? Odd questions. Strange happenings at a bus station.

A broom factory. The machinery and the process of manufacture; the annual output of the plant. The sizes of various brooms; the history of broommaking. A time-and-cost comparison between the day when brooms were made by hand and today's assembly-line operation utilizing plastics and man-made fibers.

JANUARY 24

Gold discovered in California (1848) . . . First Boy Scout troop organized, England (1908) . . . Humphrey O'Sullivan patents the rubber heel (1899).

A ghost writer. Putting words in the mouth (or under the byline) of famous persons not experienced in authorship. How speeches are ghostwritten for statesmen. How college students sometimes employ ghost writers—illegally!—to prepare their themes. The rates for ghost writing.

Mr. Chairman! Ask a parliamentarian to outline and explain the rules, traditions and terminology of a meeting. Illustrate meaning of such terms as "quorum," "point of order," "table the motion," and so on.

School for models. Spend a day at a school for models, developing story around theme that beauty isn't just there—it's worked for! Tips on cosmetics from the experts. What the girls must do, step by step. Their diet fads. New gimmicks in accessories. Fashion hints. A model's earnings.

JANUARY 25

St. Paul's Day (superstition about weather for the year, based on weather conditions this day) . . . Birth of Robert Burns (1759) . . . Shay's Rebellion (1787).

Remember the Blue Eagle? Merchants and industrialists reminisce about the National Recovery Administration (NRA) and the days of the famous blue eagle. The self-regulatory steps that were taken to help the country lift itself out of the depression.

Premiums are big business. Survey the number of free and inexpensive gifts available to a consumer who sends in *every* coupon appearing in one issue of a specific magazine, and every label (on which an offer appears) on packages displayed in the supermarket on one particular day. Discuss premium manufacturers, their sales efforts, the drive to get kids into the box-top habit.

Use of scarecrows by farmers. All about scarecrows, with comments by the county agent and the farmers themselves. Just how effective are scarecrows? What modern substitutes are now in use?

JANUARY 26

Birth of Roy Chapman Andrews (1884) . . . First hydroplane flown by G. H. Curtiss in San Diego (1911).

How a Congressman feels about mail. With an elected official, go over his daily mail; your emphasis should be on how these letters affect his decision on a key vote. Is he as impressed by a form telegram as by a handwritten note? How does he recognize "lobby" efforts? How does he answer his correspondence?

What those punched cards mean. We're all becoming increasingly aware of the card with holes punched in it and carrying a bold printed message that reads: "*Do Not Bend!*" What happens to these cards when they're returned? Interview an IBM executive for the story behind the electronic machines in wide use in business today.

A reservist goes to camp. For two weeks every year, Army reservists return to camp for training. What is their program like? How does it feel to go back to military duties after 50 weeks of civilian life? Do they lose weight, get back in shape? What new techniques are learned?

JANUARY 27

Birth of Wolfgang Amadeus Mozart (1756) and Lewis Carroll (1832) . . . First state university in U. S. chartered (Georgia, 1785) . . . Edison granted patent on incandescent light (1880).

The operation of a costume shop. Types of costumes most in demand; those now least often rented. Making every detail of a costume authentic. The wear and tear on rented costumes.

A mummy in a museum in your state. How the methods used by Egyptian embalmers have defied discovery by modern scientists. How the mummy in the museum was obtained. Does the mummy awe children more than adults?

Ambulance by air. A local aviator who frequently rushes sick people to distant places. His longest errands of mercy. Special equipment on his plane. Transfer of patients to regular ambulance. Arranging the schedule for speed.

JANUARY 28

First college daily newspaper, Yale News, *starts publication (1878) . . . Founding, U.S. Coast Guard (1915).*

Buying waste paper. Contact a paper stock company. Source of most waste paper; using paper again; prices.

Drama in education. "Plays with a purpose" staged at schools and churches; their messages; how the youngsters react; the immense amount of family fuss and excitement that goes into making little Susie a "snowflake" or little Tom one of the Wise Men.

Hands that stumped the experts. Present an assortment of bridge, poker, rummy hands that can be played several ways. How would the reader play them? Answers by local, regional or national figures known for their unusual card sense.

JANUARY 29

Birth of Thomas Paine (1737) and William McKinley (1843) . . . American League organized with eight teams (1900).

Stages in drawing ability. Schools can supply you with drawings of familiar objects as sketched by kindergartners, first-graders, and so on. Teachers, art experts, psychologists explain a child's artistic development—when arms and legs are no longer just "sticks," when perspective is seen in houses, and so on.

No fun to be an Admissions Director! Interview the man who holds this tough job at a college. The pressures to accept poor or mediocre students. Competition for entrance. His advice to parents and applicants.

Weather vanes. How this feature of bygone days has practically disappeared; vanes with interesting histories; various designs, as recalled by old-timers of the community. How early residents of the county had to serve as their own weathermen, with "signs" and the vanes as their aids in forecasting.

JANUARY 30

Birthday, Franklin D. Roosevelt (1882) . . .
Mohandas K. Gandhi assassinated (1948).

A motorcycle daredevil. Two-wheel stunts in which he risks his life—i.e., driving through a roaring inferno. Lucky and unlucky moments in his career; his most serious mishaps; his highest speeds. Does he drive a motorcycle or car when he's not entertaining?

Increase in the use of safety clothing. Slant: How the practice not only reduces factory accidents, but also increases efficiency. How the workers in a local or county factory wear goggles, helmets, safety shoes, gloves, leggings, and perhaps gas masks. Interview the safety director of the plant.

Have gypsies of today departed from the customs and traditions of their ancestors? Interview some members of a band working or wandering in your section. Modern means of livelihood—fortune-telling, for example, or "advising." How far has the band travelled during the past twelve months? The skill of the gypsies as musicians and also as dancers—past and present.

JANUARY 31

Child Labor Day . . . Birthday, Franz Schubert (1797).

Animal traps. Once home-made almost exclusively, traps of all sizes and shapes are now commercially manufactured. Show range, "humane" innovations, electronic-age techniques. Interview commercial trappers and hobbyists; discuss bounties still paid, by whom, where, and for what animals. Interview those who still make their own traps. Any "Rube Goldberg" traps you can describe and photograph?

An insight into the grand jury. How names are selected; how citizens become eligible for service on the grand jury. What are the jurors' duties and their authority?

Doll-houses. A collector talks about her prized doll-house, its furniture and furnishings, what she has made and what purchased (and where), and provides information on making your own for your daughter, granddaughter or niece. Photos of this mansion in miniature.

FEBRUARY 1

Feast of St. Brigid . . . National Freedom Day . . . First session, Supreme Court (1790) . . . Birth of Victor Herbert (1859) . . . Texas leaves Union (1859).

The county sanitarian. His multiple duties—not only inspecting sewage disposal facilities and water supplies, but also conducting inspections of food establishments and school lunchrooms. How scientific technique has become the basis of his work; his laboratory and the skilled technicians at work there.

Pet peeves of a suburban housewife. Concentrate on her trips to answer the doorbell and telephone; how she is the daily target of canvassers in civic, religious, and other drives; new gimmicks used to get her attention and pin-money. If she succumbed to all offers, what would her daily expenditures be?

Mechanic for a champion stock-car racer. The enormous responsibility of his job: step-by-step in his check-up routine; what he can tell the average driver about car up-keep; emergency repairs. Does he insist that his driver carry a good-luck token while at the wheel? Safety hints for Sunday motorists.

FEBRUARY 2

Ground-Hog Day . . . National League founded with eight teams (1876).

Father and son auctioneers. Description of typical auctions, city and country style; lingo and sign language of the auctioneer; the psychological hints passed on by father to son—how they create excitement, spot the likely buyer, wake up a dull audience.

Tricks used to prevent absenteeism. Many men's and women's clubs penalize members who do not attend their sessions. For example, some rural groups insist that absent members keep a rabbit or goat for a week or ten days. What other ruses or penalties can you uncover? What really startling innovations? One church gives green stamps. Can anyone top that? (*Should one?*)

Ground-Hog Day. What do local weathermen say about the ground-hog legend? How the legend originated with the Pennsylvania Germans; other weather beliefs and sayings handed down for generations, with a true-or-false test for readers.

FEBRUARY 3

Four Chaplains Memorial Day . . . Paper money first issued by a colony (Massachusetts, 1690) . . . Birth of Horace Greeley (1811) . . . Income tax adopted (1913).

Requests for dirt. How chambers of commerce, mayors, the governor and agriculture agents receive requests from distant states for soil samples. Why? Other similar requests for minerals, agricultural products, rocks, leaves. You can write to people making such requests, following up with them in order to show how information is used by hobbyists, students, industry, schools.

Exploding myths about your state's history. Interview the president of the state historical society concerning common misconceptions about the state's past. Historical figures seen in a fresh light; recent research that has produced interesting revelations.

Filling Civil Service positions. Facts about employment in the Civil Service. The wide range of positions to be filled locally, in the state, nation, and abroad; openings that attract the most applicants; opportunities for women, the semi-retired, the handicapped. There's always an examination going on!

FEBRUARY 4

George Washington elected President (1789) . . . Birth of Charles Lindbergh (1902) . . . Founding of USO (1941).

The county in the geographic center of your state. Its chief industries and claims to fame; government officials and their predictions for the next quarter of a century. Slant: How its central location has given the county advantages upon which industry and agriculture have capitalized.

Emergency vehicles. The work of mechanics in keeping ambulances, fire-fighting equipment, and police vehicles in running condition; the most common repairs; mechanics with the longest service; number of vehicles that must be serviced at the various centers.

The spreading family tree. From local library to nationwide advertiser, there's information available for folks who wish to trace their genealogy. Choose a few people who guide these researches into the past, showing how residents from distant states write for genealogical information, how data is acquired, how requests are handled. Give the reader "do-it-yourself" information.

FEBRUARY 5

Anniversary of the Constitution in Mexico . . . Birth of Dwight L. Moody (1837) . . . Birth of Adlai Stevenson (1900).

A pigeon farm. Pigeons have been demobilized by the military, but there is nevertheless heavy demand for these birds: squabs for table use, special types for research work, pure-breds for foundation stocks of breeders, homing pigeons. Describe the farm; when was it established? The original and present investment; the number of employees. How much food is consumed by the pigeons each day? Prices of the birds; largest orders; modern breeding techniques.

What politicians do after leaving office. Use as your news peg the retirement of an important official. Extend to cover or include Presidents, governors, mayors, kings, or district attorneys of past and present. Interview retired officials; should "elder statesmen" be used as advisers? What are various pension plans?

A veteran trainer of race horses. His career and methods of grooming, training, breeding. His best known horses.

FEBRUARY 6

Birth of Aaron Burr (1756) and William Maxwell Everts (1818) . . . Young Women's Hebrew Association organized (1902) . . . General Eisenhower named Commander-in-Chief of AEF (1943).

A collector of license plates. Slant: License tags as salesmen. Describe the state "advertising" that appears on plates. What about special license-plate collections—for bicycles, trucks, from abroad? Which plates are easiest to read? Describe collector's organizations, what they swap and with whom.

Forgotten arsenals. Have you ever wondered how many weapons there are on public squares of cities and towns in America? History of and statistics on these mortars, cannons, machine guns; how they were acquired; the oldest and the largest. Are any still used on Independence or Veterans' Day? Did any ever figure in schoolboy pranks?

Highway surveying. The work of the state highway department in mapping new routes, deciding on curves and grades, probable traffic load, likely suburban growth, etc.; the ire of some landowners who object to a change in highways, even to the point of sit-down strikes.

FEBRUARY 7

Birth of Charles Dickens (1812), Sinclair Lewis (1885) and Babe Ruth (1894).

"Brother teams." Here's an example of an idea that is adaptable for use in a small weekly newspaper or a national magazine. Locally, choose professional "brother teams"—physicians, for example; discuss their combined number of operations; most operations performed in a single day. Sidelights about their medical careers, hobbies, families. Extend by bringing in nationally-known pairs (Mayos, Crosbys, Eisenhowers), or using "sister teams," etc.

Your child's reading. Interview a children's librarian, an author of juvenile books, or a well-known editor—or all three—to get an article containing suggestions for parents. Recommended reading lists, by age and sex. Are children reading more or fewer books these days? How do libraries decide whether to buy a book?

Experiences of a government chemist. Crime is the smallest part of his job; how he protects and helps us in his day-to-day activities with foods, toys, products, water, etc. Slant: Your personal chemist guards your health and safety.

FEBRUARY 8

Birth of William Tecumseh Sherman (1820) . . . Boy Scouts formally incorporated (1910).

The bus barn in your city. A typical day: mechanics taking care of vehicles; chief causes of trouble; number of street cars or buses in use; total mileage traveled monthly; safety program by the transportation company; legends about the system.

A veteran watch-repair specialist. The most common "ills" of a watch; some of the most unusual timepieces, as well as the most expensive, worked on by the subject; the repairer's advice to watch owners.

Earliest photographs of a city. News peg: the city's birthday, a rebuilding program, or ceremonies marking the opening of an important new building. Lead into city as it was; business establishments and dwellings in old photographs that are still standing; historic sites; where pictures are kept, and how acquired; who took photographs, and why.

FEBRUARY 9

Birth of William Henry Harrison (1773) . . . U.S. weather service begun (1870) . . . French ship Normandie *burns (1942).*

Stranded travelers. If no Traveler's Aid Station is available, where do stranded or penniless travelers go for help? Get anecdotes and statistics from police stations, hospitals, Y's, schools, hotels—and try to locate a farmer who actually has sheltered a traveling salesman. (Your best approach: Try it yourself!)

Blood transfusions for dogs. Science saves many pets with transfusions. Discuss blood types, number of transfusions that can be given one dog. Where does the blood come from? Describe donors among the canine population. Excellent photo possibilities.

How a quartet of your section travels in filling engagements far and near. The longest trips to present programs; delays that almost prevented the group's appearance; bad weather as an obstacle. Do members of the families of the singers accompany them sometimes?

FEBRUARY 10

Marriage of Queen Victoria (1840) . . . Alanson Crane receives patent for fire extinguisher (1863).

A Sunday School class for mutes. Use photos to show how the Bible message is delivered in sign language. The teacher and the "translator"—their training, how they decided on their dedicated work, how they have brought their class to a "level" of knowledge. How many words "spoken" in such a class as compared with thc usual Sunday School session?

Scrapbooks. Many and varied are the memory books kept by people—collections of news items, cartoons, humor, fashions, travel, personal memorabilia, poetry. Describe and quote from them; show how they are read by relatives and friends confined by illness, or by youngsters as research for school work. Ever displayed on special occasions? Evcr of financial value?

Unusual gates at private residences and institutions. Arc some noted for their ornamental and graceful designs? Do any gates bear unusual legends? Word or photo quiz on famous entrances, doors, gates, local or international in scope.

FEBRUARY 11

Birth of Thomas Alva Edison (1847).

Indian treaties. Your state director of Indian affairs can describe some of the unusual agreements made in the early days of the nation, and still honored (sometimes more for traditional than practical reasons).

The laundry of a hospital. The equipment and number of workers; statistics on the clothes, sheets, linen washed daily. At what rate do hospital bed clothes wear out? What special sterilizing methods are required in a hospital?

Odd statues. Limited only by your research, this can be slanted locally, statewide or nationally, or by type of statue, categories, etc. For example, animal statues: a pig is on the roof of St. Patrick's Cathedral in New York. What about focussing on statues of children, Indians, farmyard animals, folklore characters? A photo feature.

FEBRUARY 12

Birth of Peter Cooper (1791), Abraham Lincoln (1809) and Charles Darwin (1809).

Predicting multiple births. Interview physicians about their experiences. Are many parents of twins or triplets completely surprised? Families with more than one set of twins. Contact hospitals, department stores, diaper services to learn the latest wrinkles in "twin insurance."

The fate of the revolving door. How many remain locally and in neighboring cities? First ones in your city, as recalled by an elderly citizen. Door innovations, including the self-opening entrance now finding particular favor in supermarkets and terminals.

Air freight. Planes now carry cargoes ranging from exotic animals to dismantled factories. Interview a traffic agent or pilot to learn the special requirements of these odd jobs, and to give insight into daily trucking along the highways of the air.

FEBRUARY 13

Founding in Boston of first public school in U.S. (1635).

We're surrounded by signs and signals! Choose one locality. Show the sea of signs and signals around us: traffic signs; rail, bus and trolley lights and markers; pedestrian signs; airline beacons. Who is responsible for their care and upkeep? Describe the constant check of equipment by town, city, state and federal departments, and private industry and the utility companies.

Favorite poems. Build your own annotated anthology of the favorite poems of selected people—i.e., Congressmen, magistrates, entertainers, teachers. Or, to give your article a news peg, ask for favorite rhymes about specified subjects—snowfall, parents, holidays, etc. Why are these poems their favorites? Any original verse they care to contribute?

First ladies of the Supreme Court of your state. Chief interests of the wives of the members of the Supreme Court. "The judge at home." Preventing overwork by their husbands; ideal vacations; social obligations of the family. Do the justices discuss cases with their wives? Who takes care of their robes?

FEBRUARY 14

St. Valentine's Day . . . Day of Commemoration (of Statehood) in Oregon . . . Arizona becomes the forty-eighth State to enter the Union (1912).

Be glad you don't run a restaurant! A restaurant manager discusses his problems: guessing what people will eat, the effects of weather on appetite, cranks, patrons who "borrow" silver and linen, food fads, dieters, undisciplined children. Slant: An anonymous, frank interview.

A handwriting expert. Is he a believer in graphology, the art of judging a person's disposition, character and even aptitudes from his handwriting? Lead from this into the uses of his work—validating signatures on wills, rare documents, the question of forgery, handwriting in cases of kidnapping, suicide.

St. Valentine's Day. The probate judge of your state who ranks as the champion "Marrying Sam." The number of years he has joined 'em in matrimony, and the number of couples he has united.

FEBRUARY 15

Birth of Galileo (1564) and Susan B. Anthony (1820) . . . Battleship Maine *explodes in Havana harbor (1898).*

Kissing at bus and train stations. Observations by attendants. Are elderly persons just as affectionate in their farewells as members of the younger generation? Is there reason to believe some smoochers are not passengers? Do any couples quarrel at the station?

Paying funeral expenses in advance. Question undertakers and funeral directors about the people who methodically prepare for death—selecting burial items, planning funeral details, writing their own epitaphs for prepaid tombstones.

"When you give a present to . . ." A minister, teacher, doctor or retiring administrator, what should it be? Quiz such people about unique gifts, "white elephants," monotonously unimaginative presents they've received. How many copies of same book, ties?

FEBRUARY 16

Birth of Henry Adams (1838) . . . Founding of Benevolent and Protective Order of Elks (1868) . . . Founding of American Society of Mechanical Engineers (1880).

A family of foreign missionaries. Your minister or a denominational headquarters can put you in touch with a family that has performed unusual missionary service. Their experiences, en route and at the mission. Hardships, rewards, anecdotes and adventures abound. Medical emergencies; successes in conversions; present service.

Identifying babies in hospitals. The camera is an important and reliable adjunct to finger- and foot-printing. How, why, when used. What other safeguards are used in hospitals? Blood tests? Name bracelets?

The seal of your state. The history of the seal, as told by a well-known historian. Who designed the seal? A description of it. Slants: Photo quiz on seals . . . seals for various political offices and departments . . . making of seals.

FEBRUARY 17

Jefferson elected over Burr to Presidency (1801) . . . Gas lights in city streets for first time (Baltimore, 1817).

Innovations in bridge building. How pre-cast concrete spans facilitate the construction of bridges, increasing capacities and reducing costs and building time while eliminating hazards. See an engineer of the state highway department for similar new developments in other areas.

Collecting autographs by mail. The collection of a local resident who has gathered scores of signatures from home and abroad with simple letters of request: the most famous names in his collection; personal messages sent along with the autographs. Who refused, and why?

Shopping stamps. Pro and con on the question, "Does the shopper really pay for these stamps through higher prices?" And other aspects—statistics on filled books redeemed for merchandise; grouping of books by members of clubs or charity groups. By the way—should a tax be paid on this "free" merchandise?

FEBRUARY 18

Jefferson Davis becomes President of Confederacy (1861) . . . Animal (a cow) flown in plane for first time (1930).

"River cities." How their natural water resources produce industries, give each city a personality of its own, aid prosperity, etc.; new industries drawn by water power as compared with those of earlier times; local and international shipping. Slants: Youngsters in a river city who hope to become sailors . . . atomic energy on the Wabash.

A Bible collection. The number of Bibles in a personal or institutional collection: the largest, smallest, oldest, rarest. Bibles in foreign languages, devotionals, concordances, hymnals.

Double weddings. Their frequency in your city, discussed by local ministers. Traditions and superstitions connected with double ceremonies. Interview couples united in double weddings decades ago; their comments now. Are ties retained with the other couple? Anniversaries celebrated together? Are they godparents of the other couple's children?

FEBRUARY 19

Knights of Pythias founded (1864) . . .
Marines land on Iwo Jima (1945).

Trademarks. The oldest in use; designers of leading trademarks; how trademarks are registered; how a trademark can become one of the most valuable assets of a company. Slant: the special world of a trademark attorney.

Packing for moving. Tips from veteran drivers and packers: proper methods of wrapping and packing various household items. When does most breakage occur—en route, in wrapping, when unpacking?

Behind the prescription counter. Spend a day with a druggist; describe the number of drugs at his disposal, his techniques and precautions in filling prescriptions; latest advances in drugs and their results, in greater ease and rapidity in treating various illnesses and diseases.

FEBRUARY 20

Post Office established (1792) . . . Toothpick manufacturing machine patented (1872).

Secrets of credit and collection managers! Techniques employed by collectors; common and uncommon alibis of debtors; letters that are effective; days of the week best for collecting. How the never-say-die spirit and cleverness of credit managers and collectors keep us honest.

World geography quiz. Educators say that we Americans know less about our own and world geography than any other educated peoples. Present a quiz—devised by a specialist—to youngsters, housewives, teachers. Ask people to give you population figures, etc. And be prepared for the worst!

Odd jobs that a colorful writer has held. Jobs in which he found adventure, plot ideas, background material for his writing, and how these actual experiences inspired stories. Extend by mentioning other authors, present and past, or by concentrating on a particular occupation popular with many authors—the sea, truck driving, teaching, law, medicine, etc.

FEBRUARY 21

Brotherhood Week . . . National Ski Association formed (1904).

Fishy tricks. A round-up of the stunts performed by some of our smarter sea-friends—dolphins, seals, walruses, and so on. Information from a local expert on experiments involving fish; what we learn from fish—for instance, the potential usefulness of algae in the diet of underprivileged peoples, space voyagers, marooned seamen.

How farm animals are named. Every cow isn't Bossie," nor is every goat "Billy." A veterinarian can explain how animals are named and registered, and the importance of this to breeders.

A day in Domestic Relations Court. Descriptions of the cases that reach this specialized courtroom; decisions; advice given by the judge; incidents that indicate that a family with problems may have been helped over a hump.

FEBRUARY 22

Birth of George Washington (1630), Frederic Chopin (1810), and James Russell Lowell (1819) . . . Prohibition Party has its first national convention (1872).

George Washington's birthday. Cities in your state that were given their name in honor of Washington and other Presidents. Who suggested these designations? The early history of the places; important celebrations in observance of the founding of the cities.

The highest dam in your state. Details of its construction; the engineers; area served by the electricity generated by the plant; the use of the lake for recreational purposes. The importance of the dam to the industrial and commercial life of the area; its role in the propagation and welfare of fish and wildlife.

Rabbit delight. The most successful rabbit shows in the state; types of rabbits featured; the foremost rabbit raisers; officers of the association of rabbit breeders in the state. Quantity of rabbit meat sold in your state; stores that sell the bulk of it; any special clientele that buys it. Is rabbit meat more or less nutritious than beef or pork?

FEBRUARY 23

Birth of Samuel Pepys (1633) and George Frederick Handel (1685) . . . Founding of first Rotary Club (Chicago, 1905) . . . First mass inoculations with Salk vaccine (1954).

Methods of memory improvement. Mnemonics, the art of training the memory, is far from new—the ancient Greeks employed mnemonic systems. Rules, rhythmic lines and other devices used by local citizens.

Dust! The housewife's scourge . . . and a serious problem from industrial and public health viewpoints. What can be done about dust at various levels; on the furniture, in the air, on the farm.

The mania for miniatures. Dwarf trees are booming in florists and nurseries, the dog-breeders find that the smaller-than-standard dogs are enjoying new popularity, the five-and-dimes sell match-box-sized copies of cars and planes. Survey "miniatures" available in a typical community; seek explanation of "midgetism" from retailers, veterinarians, psychologists.

FEBRUARY 24

Birth of Winslow Homer (1836) . . . Republican Party started (Ripon, Wisconsin, 1854) . . . First multi-stage rocket fired at White Sands, New Mexico (1949).

History of the Governor's mansion in your state. Construction dates and costs; the architect; the first occupant; antiques, unusual furnishings; memorable occasions in the mansion, including banquets. Have Presidents been entertained there? Other visiting dignitaries? Slant: A long-time employee there—butler, housekeeper, gardener.

An ex-circus barker. Barkers' jargon. Rip-roaring experiences under the Big Top; circus performers of prominence whom he knows; how he makes use of his talking ability today. Does he long to return to circus activities?

Interview a detective on an arson squad. A baffling case of arson he has solved, with a step-by-step description of the clues, the search, the trial. His suggestions on arson prevention.

FEBRUARY 25

Birth of Auguste Renoir (1841) . . . Income tax amendment (16th) ratified (1913).

Typewriter repairman at work. His hints on keeping typewriters in working order; the leading keyboard troubles and how to prevent them; special problems of repairing typewriters used by neophytes in typing classes. Do women take better care of typewriters than do men? Typewriter improvements within recent years; special machines—foreign language, for the blind, for the handicapped.

Feats of an expert marksman. A virtuoso marksman demonstrates his skill. Hitting the target in various ways with the aid of mirrors, blindfolded, shooting over his shoulder. The most difficult shots—how executed, how devised, how long practiced. Describe national and international rivalry in marksmanship. Any rivalry between such arms of the law as state and city police or T-men and the FBI?

What nurses do when off duty. Means of recreation; social activities; preferences in reading matter. The nurses' concept of an ideal boy friend.

FEBRUARY 26

Birth of Victor Hugo (1802) and William "Buffalo Bill" Cody (1846).

Unusual inquiries. Interview receptionists, switchboard operators, cashiers, librarians to form a list of odd questions and requests they've had—for example, a theatre cashier is queried about movie-star marriages, a librarian is asked to settle a bet.

Portrait of a roller skating club. The number of members; ages and professions represented; the youngest skaters in the group; how and where they practice; the most difficult feats to perform. What do the members think of ice skating as a sport? Has television coverage of slam-bang skating races helped or hurt skating's popularity?

Bible salesmen still travel. Bookselling began with itinerant Bible salesmen, and they still cover the country. Interview salesmen who visit your locale—both the door-to-door salesman and representatives of large publishing houses. Are most Bibles purchased during the Christmas season? Describe special Bibles—family, wedding, military.

FEBRUARY 27

Birth of Henry Wadsworth Longfellow (1807).

Fate of the shoe-shine boy and the candy seller in railroad stations. Has "automation" decreased their number and income? Statistics to indicate the popularity of vending machines at terminals. Extend to include the new service machines—those selling insurance, reprint books, foods ranging from beef bouillon to nuts.

Valuables thrown away with trash. Talk with the head of the sanitation department. Describe searches of trash piles and the city dump; remarkable finds. Does anyone habitually explore the city dump for valuables?

Poultry research. An insight into an experimental station in your state: feeding experiments; increasing egg production; the station's director and his predictions about poultry in the next decade. Slant: How the poultry industry is meeting the challenge of increasing food requirements as the nation's population rises.

FEBRUARY 28

Birth of Linus Pauling (1901) . . . Basketball game televised for first time (New York City, 1940).

Visiting the fire and police departments. How students and such youth groups as the Scouts make tours of municipal departments. What interests the visitors most of all; leading questions they ask; the busiest visiting periods. Does the brass pole in the fire department still reign as the center of attention there?

A woman mail carrier. She makes her R.F.D. rounds despite all kinds of weather. Her total mileage per month; an estimate of the pieces of mail delivered daily; what she feels are the real rewards of her work.

Last fatal duel in your state. Public reaction to the death; dueling victims in your state through the years. Did political spats or romantic entanglements lead to many of the duels? When was dueling outlawed?

FEBRUARY 29

Leap Year . . . Birth of Gioacchino Rossini (1792).

Occupational therapy at a tuberculosis sanatorium. How such activities as printing, bookbinding, pottery making and weaving not only help patients adjust themselves to their stay but often provide them with a new vocation.

The nightly cost of street lighting in your city. How long does the average bulb last? Who (or what) turns the lights on and off? What safety measures are in use? The number of bulbs used annually; men involved in lighting; wiring; repair crews.

A law enforcement officer well known for his lectures. An estimate of the number of addresses he has given in the interest of crime prevention; longest trips to make appearances. Does he prefer talking to young people or to adults? Why does he make these speeches? Who pays him? Why? His views on juvenile delinquency.

MARCH 1

State Day in Nebraska . . . Red Cross Month . . . American colonies adopt Articles of Confederation (1781) . . . Sixteenth Amendment (income tax) becomes effective (1913).

A forest nursery. Growing seedlings and selling them to residents of the state at cost. The part played by the nursery in checking soil erosion and making the land fertile again.

An interview with a firearms examiner of a Federal Bureau of Investigation office. The process of comparing cartridges; the bullet file; exchange of ballistic information nationally and internationally.

A dialect society. Research work by the members; the best known experts on dialect who belong to the society; a typical meeting. Examples of odd dialects; the strangest dialects in the state.

MARCH 2

Texas Independence Day . . . Birth of DeWitt Clinton (1769) and Sam Houston (1793) . . . U.S. Department of Education created (1867).

Tilting tournaments as highlights of county fairs. The stiff competition among riders who strive to pierce the ring with the lance. Slant: How the colorful ceremony honoring the fair ladies combines the sport and romance of days when "knighthood was in flower."

Unusual parties. Quiz prominent hostesses for a feature dealing with entertainment that is pleasantly different: party games, unique themes, parties for youngsters, teen-age entertaining, holiday dishes.

Epidemic! Fortunately it has been many years since epidemics swept the nation. From a public health official in your area, learn the facts about an epidemic that raged in your community (city, state, region)—fatalities, unusual work by physicians and nurses, causes and cures, new techniques that prevent repetition.

MARCH 3

In Japan, "Feast of the Dolls" . . . Birth of Alexander Graham Bell (1847) . . . Premier of Birth of a Nation *(1915).*

Stay off the tracks! Interview veteran railroad engineers about obstructions on tracks; for instance, people who fall asleep there, cars that stall, kids at play, animals that wander onto the rails. Maintaining a constant check on tracks. Pictures—early cowcatchers, the "people baskets" once in vogue.

A flying family. At a local airport you're sure to meet a family where ma, pa, and perhaps even the kids have licenses. The youngest and the oldest "birds" in the family. When and why they took up flying; where they go; who has what chores—for plane upkeep, when in the air, on take-offs and landings.

A woman "outdoorsman." Slant: this woman is just as much at home in the Great Outdoors as in the kitchen. Her record in hunting (fishing, trapping, etc.). Attitude toward her trophies shown by her friends of both sexes. Photographs.

MARCH 4

Original Inauguration Day . . . Birth of Knute Rockne (1888) . . . U.S. Department of Commerce established (1913).

Wives of amateur and professional magicians. Do the wives help their husbands develop new tricks? How one wife helps in the act; her "backstage" role —for example, care of the proverbial rabbit and other animals and props. Anecdotes about impromptu shows and charity appearances. Is she ever accused of bridge-table sleight-of-hand?

Historic land deeds in county courthouses. Land deals that made history long ago, but are now forgotten; property prices in pioneer days; original owners of land on which your city now stands.

Use of photography by the medical profession. Slant: Photographs and motion pictures as permanent visual records for physicians and surgeons. How pictures are taken of difficult operations or rare conditions; special training needed by medical photographers, and any unusual equipment they use. Who sees the films? Who pays for them? How widely are prints distributed? Must the patient approve?

MARCH 5

Boston Massacre (1770) . . . Samuel Colt receives patent for his pistol (1836) . . . Depression "bank holiday" begins (1933) . . . Josef Stalin dies (1953).

Pigeon racing. Interview a local fancier about raising homing pigeons, and the pleasures of this form of racing. The speed of the pigeon in flight.

War brides revisited. These many years after World War II, how are the girls our GI's brought home? Interview several: have they visited their former homes since? Lost or retained their accents? Are they active citizens? Do they try to teach customs of the old country to their children?

An executive training program. A report by a business leader who has attended one of the intensive courses given for executives by such groups as the American Management Association. What he learned; his rigorous program; how he has put his new insights to work.

MARCH 6

Alamo Day in Texas . . . Magellan Day in Guam . . . Birth of Elizabeth Barrett Browning (1806).

A school of taxidermy. Number of present students; common (and uncommon) animals "stuffed." Where most of the animals are obtained; main points in training; the most difficult phases of the technique to master. Is the head of the school, or are any students, enthusiastic hunters?

"My favorite city from the sky." Question the leading aviators of your city. What things about various cities impress the fliers most? Slant: How many citizens never think of the "from-the-sky" appearance of their city.

Suggestion boxes. Leading businesses and plants in your city that encourage and reward employee ideas. What prizes are awarded? The best of the ideas and consequent savings in time and expense. Any patents resulting from suggestions? Adoptions of any of the ideas on a national scale.

MARCH 7

Birth of Luther Burbank (1849) . . . Alexander Graham Bell receives patent for first telephone (1876).

"I was an intelligence agent." Interview a veteran of World War II who served in the C.I.C. or C.I.D. His duties and exploits, the rigorous training, exciting and exacting cases.

"Write a composition about . . ." Prevail upon a third- or fourth-grade teacher to let you quote from compositions submitted by the youngsters. Their blunders, imaginative prose and fresh viewpoint make enticing reading.

A university press. The editorial director and his assistants. The first books and their authors; number of volumes published annually; the variety of subjects; autograph parties; the books that have enjoyed highest sales. Slant: How university presses make possible the publication of books of special significance to their states.

MARCH 8

Birth of Oliver Wendell Holmes, Jr. (1841) . . . First state law for licensing dogs (New York, 1894).

How Johnny is learning to read. What methods are in use in your community? The old "phonic" method, "word recognition," or a blend of the two? How successful? Ideas about the method, pro and con, by teachers, reading consultants. How parents can help.

Cowboy slang. You might not know it from the Westerns on TV, but cowboys have a rich jargon of their own. Interview a man who has worked on the ranches to get some of the tangy expressions in common use.

The changing "personals" column. Compare the "personals" and other classified advertising of today with that of earlier years. What about the "personals" columns of European and English newspapers, filled with really intimate and truly personal ads—for example, seeking marriage partners and friends of the opposite sex?

MARCH 9

Albert Potts receives patent for first street letterbox (1858) . . . Battle of Monitor *and* Merrimac *(1862).*

An interview with a veteran train dispatcher. How he controls the movement of trains: knowing the location of each train at all times; recording the trains' progress on a chart; issuing train orders; how automation has changed the dispatcher's work routine.

A school dietitian. If she could speak to each child's mother, what advice would she give? Her comments on common faults in nutrition; her attitudes on candy, vitamins, soft drinks; the nutritional gaps she tries to fill.

A visit to a tannery. Step by step in tanning hides; interesting information concerning skins; sources of hides; new uses of leather in the home, in automobiles, in clothing.

MARCH 10

U.S. issues its first paper currency (1862) . . . A Salvation Army contingent from London lands in New York (1880), holds first street meetings.

When you have a complete medical examination. A general practitioner or internist explains all the steps in a thorough physical check-up, showing what he learns from each test, thump, probe and question. Importance of a regular, complete physical.

Phrenology and physiognomy. Interview a devotee or a student who can explain how to "read" heads and faces. This was once a popular way to judge character and was considered truly scientific.

A dress factory. How dresses are made; the evolution of a dress from a pattern and mere cloth; the machinery.

MARCH 11

Death of John "Johnny Appleseed" Chapman (1847) . . . U.S. Army Corps of Engineers established.

Going around with a square dance caller. The number of dances a week at which he "calls"; changes in his patter, now that more city-folk, neophytes and children attend these dances. Instructions in basic steps. What about sales of records—is "automation" now entering the professional scene, or are records bought primarily for home use? How do you learn this trade? What does it pay?

Slips of the tongue of prominent speakers. Their most embarrassing boners and how they were passed off; slips on radio and television by announcers and entertainers. Slant: "Correcting the record" in courts, legislatures, the local press.

Century-old newspapers. Describe contents of newspapers published 100 years ago. Early newspaper advertising; the editors and their politics; contributors; outstanding events chronicled. Are any of these papers still published? Where can old papers be seen?

MARCH 12

First parachute jump from airplane (Captain Albert Berry, 1912) . . . Girl Scouts founded (Georgia, 1912).

Helpful hints by dry cleaners and laundrymen. "First aid" treatment for various stains; proper storage; how to "hang" garments; how chemicals can "fix" stains into clothing unless cleaner is warned; how to fold clothes for storage.

Photographing school kids. Interview a photographer who takes many graduation and class pictures. His most amusing experiences; best methods of obtaining proper poses; dealing with "hams." How profitable is his business?

Would-be brides and grooms who change their minds at the altar. How frequent are such last-minute reversals? Ostensible reasons for such actions. Experiences of local ministers in facing these crises.

MARCH 13

Birth of Joseph Priestly (1733) . . . Chester Greenwood granted patent for earmuffs (1877).

Keeping the exterior of a church clean. How often are the churches of your city painted or sand-blasted? Most common repairs made to church exteriors. Discuss the specialized companies that clean churches, municipal buildings, hospitals.

Where to turn for legal aid. How persons financially unable to pay a lawyer may receive free help from their local Legal Aid Society. Profile the officers of one local society and its staff attorneys. Number of cases handled since its inception. Extend to state and national scene: what other sources of help are available?

"No Visitors" signs. Do people obey signs? Select a site and see—at a zoo, park or hospital. How about the enforcement of such signs—and the resulting complications? For example, hospital "Hours of Visiting" rules—how relatives of patients not infrequently "raise Cain" when reminded of the rules. And what about "Wet Paint" notices?

MARCH 14

Eli Whitney patents cotton gin (1794) . . . Birth of Albert Einstein (1879) . . . First national bird reservation established (Florida, 1903).

Today's Annie Oakleys. Women marksmen in schools, clubs, law-enforcement groups. Popularity of skeet-shooting; fashions for sports women; women on safaris.

Tombstone inscriptions. Contact a tombstone dealer. The longest inscriptions he can recall; the most common inscriptions and verses; humorous or touching inscriptions from the past.

The various uses of sawdust. Interview lumber experts about the sale of sawdust for packing, insulation material, fuel, floor-sweeping compounds, briquettes and other purposes. Other "waste" products that started new industries.

MARCH 15

Ides of March . . . Birth of Andrew Jackson (1767) . . . Founding of American Legion (Paris, 1919).

Testing eyesight at the highway department. Applicants for driving licenses who are surprised to find they have defective vision. The percentage of applicants who need glasses. How about youngsters taking student-driver lessons? Contrasting state rules on eyesight. What do officials think about regular check-ups for drivers?

Interview with a college housemother. Is the "younger generation" really different? How does she keep up with changing fads? How do the real mothers fail in their duties? What are her major problems? How to handle homesick youngsters; the number of students to whom she has played Mother in her present capacity.

The oldest member of the state Supreme Court. His length of service as a member of the body; chief justices under whom he has served; memorable decisions rendered by the court since his appointment; famous cases he and fellow justices have reviewed.

MARCH 16

Birth of James Madison (1751) . . . U. S. Military Academy established (West Point, 1802).

The domestic life of midgets. Interview midgets residing in or visiting your area. Is their furniture diminutive? What are their problems in obtaining clothes?

A photoengraving plant. How engravings are made for newspaper and magazine use, as explained by the engraver. Latest improvements in engraving processes; rushing engravings to meet the deadline.

Adult education. Slant: There's no excuse for "not knowing," for adult courses are now given in subjects ranging from accounting to zoölogy. Survey of educational opportunities for adults in a community, city or state; stories about particularly diligent students; self-improvement case histories; offbeat courses demanded by adults.

MARCH 17

St. Patrick's Day . . . Evacuation Day in Boston and Suffolk County, Massachusetts . . . First U.S. glider flight (600 feet) made by J. J. Montgomery (California, 1884).

Prayer phones in your section. Number of calls each month. How often are the prayers changed? Are they prepared and spoken by ministers? Letters of appreciation.

Nature trail. These wooded paths, often bordered by a delightful stream, are sanctuaries where children and adults can observe unusual birds, small animals, striking vegetation. With camera, let your readers join you on a ramble down the trail.

Indian names. This subject can be covered on a local or national basis. The history and traditions behind Indian place names: what are their definitions? How have they changed in pronunciation? Stories of tribes that gave us these designations for rivers, mountains, valleys, towns and cities.

MARCH 18

Patent for street gas lights granted to David Melville (1813) . . . Birth of Grover Cleveland (1837).

The chaplain of a House of Representatives. His ministerial career, and his length of service as the House's chaplain; how the political scene affects his tenure, his invocations; ministers who have become politicians, and vice versa.

The telephone operators at local police headquarters. Exciting moments for the persons on duty at the police switchboard. The busiest hours. Have any women been assigned to duty as police telephone operators?

Lefties. Interview celebrities and ordinary folk about life as a lefty; special scissors, pens, etc., for our left-handed citizens; their gripes and advances. How many train themselves to become ambidextrous? Latest medical and psychological views on subject.

MARCH 19

Birth of Albert Pinkham Ryder (1847) and William Jennings Bryan (1860).

A typical day in the life of a congressman's secretary. The joys and problems of the job—soothing irate constituents, for example. Do many constituents pay visits to the congressman in Washington? Her suggestions for a child's visit to the Capitol; what adults should see; the many ways in which her office can help.

Bride's first week in cooking. From municipal records, select the names of couples married just a year ago. How did they fare at the stove during that first week of cooking? Did the bridegrooms help out in the preparation of meals? Has their cooking improved? Their favorite "quick" recipes; the prize "sad" story.

Hunting with a camera. The thrills of wildlife photography. Methods, including unending patience, special lenses and baited mechanisms to actuate the camera. The best pictures taken by an enthusiast in your section, and how they were snapped; his equipment and costs.

MARCH 20

Birth of Henrik Ibsen (1828) . . . Publication of Uncle Tom's Cabin *(1852).*

Singing schools. Why haven't voice schools kept pace in popularity with schools that offer instruction in dancing, playing musical instruments, etc.? Who are today's pupils—children, adults who sing for pleasure, professionals? What about sales of sheet music? Are we becoming a nation of "listeners"? Interview members of association of singing teachers for answers. Will "Sing-alongs" reverse the trend?

An interview with the traffic manager of a bus company. The dependence of a large segment of any city's population on its bus system. The matter of arranging the best routes; keeping the buses on schedule; "franchises"; what happens when the city's population centers move; how shopping habits affect his work.

Old streets. How they received their names; oldest houses situated on them; the city's (state's, country's) narrowest city streets; those with the most twists and turns; steepest lanes. Special streets—for example, where gaslights are retained; streets turned into malls.

MARCH 21

Vernal Equinox . . . George Washington commissions first naval officer of U.S. (Hopley Yeaton, 1791) . . . Birth of Johann Sebastian Bach (1865).

A young geologist. Profile of a youngster who collects rocks, pebbles, stones; what stirred his interests originally; what new friendships and knowledge he has gained; his most unusual stones; those from areas most distant from him. Slant: This lad knows we walk on treasure (history, oil, etc.).

Farewell notes. When death or departure is imminent, messages are often written—farewells, advice, revelations, confessions. Compare farewell notes of the famed and the little-known; those of great historical significance; humorous farewells; notes in museums and public buildings.

Theater marquees. The step-by-step job of changing the marquee legends whenever the program changes. Humorous mistakes in marquee spelling, and the wry effects of listing double features. Extend by asking the managers about the most effective types of ballyhoo methods outside the theater—displays, "pickets," sound, caged animals, etc.

MARCH 22

Emancipation Day in Puerto Rico . . . Patent for cornstarch granted to O. Jones (1841) . . . Founding of Young Men's Hebrew Association (YMHA) in New York (1874).

"Just married" signs. Make this an interview with hotel, motel and service station operators. Difficulties in removing signs and lettering from automobiles. Is the stringing of cans to cars still practiced? Do signs and practical jokes lead to quarrels? Ask local psychologist to comment on this tradition.

Unruly passengers. Instances in which ambulance, cab and bus drivers—and airline pilots—were taxed in their strength and patience by disorderly or hysterical passengers. Lead into this with report on pertinent new legislation, special training developments or a safety expert's statement.

Snowfalls. Is the annual snowfall rate really decreasing? What months have produced the greatest snowfalls? Discuss snow as big business—removal equipment, chemicals, artificial-snow machines, snow tires. Show effect of snow on one typical community's finances.

MARCH 23

Patrick Henry's "Liberty or Death" speech (1775) . . . Tennessee enacts law against teaching Darwin's theory of evolution (1925).

Growing popularity of model railroading among girls. Retailers and hobbyist clubs can lead you to girls who possess extensive model train collections. Many daughters of railroad employees follow this hobby; girls often design unusually detailed "scenery" for their trains. A good photo-feature.

An interview with a rare-book dealer. How he gathers the books; his oldest and rarest volumes; old books in great demand; the process of finding books wanted by collectors, illustrated by the search for one unusual volume.

Shiny money! Hotels and business establishments in your section that indulge in the practice of cleaning coins: the process and cost and time required; old coins discovered during the cleaning process; hotels giving out new currency only.

MARCH 24

Virginia enacts first colonial game law (1629) . . . Independence of the Philippine Islands granted (1934).

"Joiners." Choose one or more political leaders—the mayor, for example—to show how "joining" and "politicking" go together. Subject's service in the clubs; the value of the clubs, in his estimation; the most unusual clubs of which he has been a member.

Photography as a hobby or business with local aviators. "Discovering" your city and its most impressive features via the camera. The best time of day for aerial photography; types of cameras; striking pictures taken from the sky; uses of aerial photography.

Local cops who rank as favorites with children. How about fat policemen who are unusually popular with kids? Officers' acts of kindness toward boys and girls; their role in preventing vandalism, delinquency; youth associations headed by police officials.

MARCH 25

Maryland Day . . . Birth of Arturo Toscanini (1867) . . . Coxey's Army begins march on Washington (1894).

A modern "village smithy." His work in this rubber-tire era. Duties other than shoeing mules and horses—for instance, repairing farm machinery. His busiest seasons. Does *he* consider horseshoes "lucky"?

Opening locked cars. Are women or men more forgetful when it comes to locking automobiles and leaving the keys inside? Methods of solving the predicament, other than smashing a window. Any infants or pets accidentally locked into cars?

A modern quarry. Quarrying was once an exceedingly dangerous occupation, but modern techniques have almost eliminated accidents among workers. The processes employed in quarrying; the various pieces of equipment; safety precautions; markets for the products.

MARCH 26

Kuhio Day in Hawaii . . . Birth of Robert Frost (1875) . . . Death of Walt Whitman (1892) . . . Salk Vaccine announced (1953).

Bugs. How to tell friend from foe among farm insects (get your information from your local extension service agent). "Seasons" for bugs in your region, and latest insecticides. Special aspects of insects in modern America: ladybugs are sold by the bucket to farmers, and ant colonies are a popular hobby. Legends about insects: some signal storms or dry periods, for example.

Heart surgery. A major hospital can provide the latest information on new forms of heart repair—including "freezing," "blocking," removal of calcified areas, diet information. Dramatic examples abound: surgery to save youngsters, emergency heart massaging. Tie in with heart-fund drive or additions to hospital.

Applications. Check admissions directors of colleges, personnel directors, employment advisers on the do's and don'ts of application forms and letters. Show samples of effective applications.

MARCH 27

Ponce de Leon discovers Florida (1513) . . . Birth of Nathaniel Currier (1813) . . . M. L. Byrn granted patent for corkscrew (1860).

Tropical fish collections. This can be as local as the foremost hobbyist in town, or can be extended to include today's big business in tropical fish. Hints for successful care and breeding; the cost of rare tropicals; an aquarium for children that can "grow," species by species. Local and national societies; swapping fish; strange habits of tropicals (some practice cannibalism of offspring, females kill males, etc.).

A well-known bird painter. How he familiarized himself with bird life; his visits to wildlife refuges; selling his paintings; interesting bird habits he notices while at work. His techniques at work—does he use photographs, rough sketches or caged models?

The most disastrous hotel fires in your state's history. Causes of the blazes; the number of persons who lost their lives; thrilling rescues; the saving of valuables by hotel patrons. How old were the hotels? Were some of them rebuilt?

MARCH 28

Senate censures President Andrew Jackson for "assuming authority and power not conferred by Constitution" (1834).

Illnesses on trains. Recollections of veteran conductors. Most common sicknesses. Do many persons become train sick? Has the stork ever paid visits on the train? Emergency cases handled by the conductor.

An old water mill of your county. How long has it been grinding corn? Slant: The former importance of water mills in the life of a community.

A hospital for handicapped children. Illnesses and deformities that once meant a life of despair can now be treated successfully. Describe latest methods of treatment; discuss "graduates" of the hospital who live normal, happy, productive lives. How are children as patients? What special problems? Cover unusual equipment for physical therapy, etc.

MARCH 29

Birth of John Tyler (1790) . . . First federal highway (Great National Pike) authorized (1806) . . . Niagara Falls stops flowing for 30 hours (1848).

Guns of noted hunters of your county. Do any of the guns have "nicknames"? Pointers on firearms and hunting; record "bags" of the nimrods; hunting laws in the state.

Hand language. How mutes and deaf-mutes converse through hand language. Photographs of sample sentences in hand language; other aids to normal living for the handicapped, such as typewriters for the blind (Braille playing cards are a recent innovation).

Vehicle manager of a local U.S. Post Office. The all-important role of trucks in fulfilling the pledge that the mail will go through, despite weather obstacles. Common repairs needed; number of tires used; mechanics with the longest records of service; safety records of drivers.

MARCH 30

Seward's Day in Alaska . . . First operation with patient under general anaesthesia (1842) . . . Birth of Vincent Van Gogh (1853) . . . Alaska purchased from Russia (1867).

When's the next eclipse? Readers will be surprised to learn how frequently there are eclipses to be seen from various parts of this planet. A local observatory may be making plans right now for one in the future. What do we learn from these events in the sky? Recount stories of eclipses that were deemed "the end of the world."

Embroidery—even more difficult than it seems! Testimony by an expert on various aspects of this needlework art: embroidery by machine, monograms, simple design, Chinese design, counted thread embroidery, embroidery on church vestments. Are youngsters taking up the art?

Speech teachers. The term no longer refers primarily to the "elocution teacher," but to therapists who do astonishing work with retarded, palsied, and otherwise handicapped children, and with adults who stutter and stammer. Show the work of a speech therapist, her training, the slow and patient techniques she uses. Case histories of successes.

MARCH 31

Transfer Day in the Virgin Islands . . . Birth of Franz Joseph Haydn (1732) . . . First vote by a Negro (New Jersey, 1870) . . . Daylight Saving Time inaugurated (1918).

Chemical gardening. A local citizen who follows this fascinating hobby. Things that can be grown without soil; how the subject learned the hobby; information about hydroponics.

Boys and girls who print neighborhood newspapers. The frequency of the issues; how the newspapers are printed; the number of reporters; "scoops" by the editorial staff; the circulation managers and their efforts; the subscription rates.

How good are local citizens at giving directions? Try out a dozen or so men and women on uptown streets. Are some more courteous than others? Do people feel impelled to give directions even when they're uncertain? Does *everyone* say "You can't miss it"?

APRIL 1

April Fool's Day . . . First colonial treaty with Indians (Plymouth, 1621) . . . First scheduled night passenger flight leaves New Jersey for Boston (1927).

April Fool's Day. Pranks of long ago, as recalled in old newspaper and magazine features. Illustrate with old cartoons and drawings. Try to trace one favorite stunt back through the years—for example, the empty pocketbook or the purse on a string.

Tornado cities. Damage by tornadoes. Tornado oddities. Are storm cellars still popular? How we meet the threat of tornadoes today.

Excuses given to school teachers. Are some of the excuses too fantastic to believe? Catching up with fibbers. What are some of the stock excuses? Which excuses are foolproof.

APRIL 2

Birth of Hans Christian Andersen (1805) and Emile Zola (1840) . . . Patent for aluminum granted to C. M. Hall (1889).

Tree houses. All kids love a "private place" up in a tree. Photos and diagrams of typical youngster's clubhouses above the ground; how to make one and how to make it safe.

Motors that you can make. Playthings for children that move; motors made with paper clips, batteries, wire; using steam or wind; rubber-band motors; combustion engines for model planes. Use photos of motors actually designed by youngsters in a science class, with "do-it-yourself" directions.

An interview with a sidewalk photographer. His technique in photographing persons on downtown streets. Who are his best customers—men, women or children? The average number of persons he snaps daily.

APRIL 3

Birth of Washington Irving (1783) . . . Pony Express inaugurated (1860) . . . Jesse James shot and killed (1882).

Telephone bills. The billing department's operations—and the parade of life witnessed by the employees month in and month out. Are most patrons prompt in their payments? Are many telephones disconnected because of non-payment?

Speaker's water pitchers. Do speakers really ever drain their pitchers of water during a speech? Or are these traditional fixtures just an invitation to mishaps? Have they been used in legislatures to stall a vote? Or as weapons? Do they ever contain liquids somewhat stronger than H_2O?

An interview with the operator of a newspaper clipping service. How a local clipping bureau cuts stories from publications and sells them to companies, individuals, institutions. The charge for their services; investment; staff. Services specialize in particular kinds of clientele—publishing, business, government—any other specialities? Slant: income for the handicapped or semi-retired.

APRIL 4

Birth of Dorothea Lynde Dix (1802) . . . Tyler becomes first vice-president to succeed to Presidency through death (1841) . . . U.S. declares war on Germany (1917).

Garbage collectors and dogs. Slant: Postmen are not the only public servants who must face the perils of unfriendly animals. Annoyances and attacks suffered by the trash removers. Any special way to lull a menacing canine into friendliness?

They'll tell your fortune! Extent of sales of horoscope material at newsstands and bookstores. Other "readers of the future"—tea-leaf readers, astrologers, palmists, etc. Slant: gather and list all the conflicting (or agreeing?) predictions about one day in your (or someone else's) week.

Street scene. Total street mileage; longest and shortest streets; streets with the longest and shortest names; streets named in honor of women; street markers; streets bearing misspelled names.

APRIL 5

Pocahontas marries John Rolfe (1614) . . . Birth of Sir Joseph Lister (1827) and Booker T. Washington (1856).

Hope chests, today and yesterday. Compare the young girl of today with her counterpart in earlier days. Use recollections, diary quotes, information from the local historical society to picture the contents of early American hope chests.

Fur farms. Interview breeders of fur-bearing animals: a visit to a mink or chinchilla farm; hardships of the work and its rewards; how the mink goes from farm to *salon*.

Is chivalry dead? Interview women about the gallantries (or lack of them) men show today. What courtesies are most appreciated? Which are rarely extended? What have been their experiences while traveling?

APRIL 6

Patent for coffee mill granted to J. Carrington (1829) . . . Founding of Mormon Church (1830) . . . Peary reaches North Pole (1909).

Cigar bands and labels. Interview a collector: how did he get started? Why? Does his collection have any financial value? What does his family think about it? What rarities does he still seek? Unusual facts about "smokers, stickers and segars."

The work of a parole board. Seeking to maintain good morale at the penitentiary; compelling problems; reducing terms for good behavior; how applicants for parole are judged. How long are parolees under surveillance?

What's good for hiccoughs? How about airplane rides? Superstitions; nostrums; photographs of unusual positions and stunts recommended as "sure cures"; comments by a physician about remedies he has used.

APRIL 7

Birth of William Wordsworth (1770) . . .
Opening of South Pacific *(1949).*

Marked money. How law enforcement officers solve crimes through the use of marked money. An estimate of how speedily money changes hands. Do local officers make frequent use of the marked money system? "Marked money" used for community public relations—such as factory workers paid in silver dollars to demonstrate financial importance of the factory in the area.

Veteran officials who have missed only a few (if any) days on the job in many years. How they stay in good health; their prescriptions for promptness. Contrast their records with statistics on absenteeism. The public offices held by these men and women; interesting anecdotes about the occasions when they were tempted to stay away from their jobs, and why they were glad they had not done so.

What firemen save at blazes. A group of fire-fighters recalls humorous incidents in saving household articles and pets. The items that people carry out of a burning home or rush back to rescue.

APRIL 8

First dental clinic for the poor incorporated (New York City, 1795) . . . Birth of Harvey William Cushing (1869).

Operations of a central credit bureau in your city. Furnishing credit information to merchants; obtaining the data; out-of-the-ordinary experiences in connection with the bureau.

The dean of boxing referees in your state. The most thrilling bouts he has refereed; shortest matches he has witnessed; outstanding instances of sportsmanship among boxers.

Noted athletes as operators of businesses. Slant: How farsighted athletes, realizing that their money-making years in sports may be limited, open such establishments as cafes and sporting goods stores. Are athletes good businessmen? The most successful such enterprise, offset by anecdotes of businesses that failed.

APRIL 9

Founding of first tax-supported public library (Peterborough, N.H.) in U.S. (1833) . . . Bataan falls (1942).

Providing ample water for industrial uses in your state. Slant: How plentiful supplies of water form a big lure for factories; expanding waterworks; water projects; daily consumption of water in the largest cities in the state.

When things go down the drain. Frantic searches for rings and other valuables, as reported by plumbers. How far have some articles traveled before they were recovered?

A state press photographer's association. This group can help you build dozens of photo features—it means sales for them as well as for you. Hints on posing and lighting; animal pictures; "composite" of most beautiful girl; most exciting pictures of their careers; amusement park sequences; "the picture that got away."

APRIL 10

First issue of New York Herald *(1841) . . . Birth of Joseph Pulitzer (1847) . . . Safety pin patented by Joseph Hunt (1849).*

A sword collection. The swords with the most colorful histories; the largest, oldest, the very unusual (those hidden in canes, for example).

An interview with a widely-known geologist. The science of investigating the earth's structure; some of the geologist's most important findings.

Injunctions. What they are, how obtained, how long effective; how the reader can be enjoined against using property, entering certain businesses, putting up a new building, spending inherited money, and so on.

APRIL 11

Birth of Charles Evans Hughes (1862) . . . Spanish-American War ends (1899) . . . Jackie Robinson first Negro in major league baseball (1947).

Popular names. The registrar of births will permit you to survey the first names given the current crop of babies. What names are newly popular? What old-fashioned names seem to be making a comeback? The "meanings" of some popular names.

Etchings—how they're made. Interview an artist who specializes in etchings. Show the painstaking process, step-by-step, illustrated by photographs and the prints themselves.

The laws of evidence. A lawyer explains what courts consider evidence, what the cop on the beat or the detective must know, why a judge will not "accept" certain forms of evidence, and what the reader should know about the subject if he is ever involved in a crime or accident.

APRIL 12

Anniversary of passage of Halifax Independence Resolution in North Carolina . . . Birth of Henry Clay (1777) . . . First railroad tunnel (Johnstown to Hollidaysburg, Pennsylvania) begun (1831) . . . Firing on Fort Sumter (1861) . . . Death of Franklin D. Roosevelt (1945).

Vocational tests. All around us—in schools, industry, business, hospitals—vocational tests are being given to young and old. Show how in one community these psychological techniques are used to help people find the right career.

"Accounting for the housewife." A leading CPA can show how sound business rules work at home—in managing the checkbook, making buying decisions, saving on taxes, putting money aside for the future.

Our "bouncing nation." "Trampolines" are a recent fad; interview gymnasts or acrobats or physical training instructors to look back at other favorite bouncing games and stunts—chinning-bars and punching bags from the Twenties, tumbling, balancing, group gymnastics.

APRIL 13

Memorial Day in Nebraska . . . Birth of Thomas Jefferson (1743) . . . First elephant to arrive in America lands (New York, 1796) and is put on exhibit . . . Birth of Frank W. Woolworth (1852).

The oldest house still standing in your county. Its original owner and its fate through the years; its condition today and the present occupant; relics in the dwelling.

Kind letters received by the local police department. How out-of-towners thank the officers for their courtesy, especially in giving information and directions. Slant: The valuable service of policemen as a sort of information bureau.

Slogans of cities in your state. How they originated; distinctive qualities of the cities; how slogans are used to attract tourists and expand business and industrial life.

APRIL 14

Pan American Day . . . Founding of first society against slavery (Philadelphia, 1775) . . . Publication of Noah Webster's Dictionary *(1828).*

A day at an auction for automobile dealers. Sources of the cars; number of dealers generally in attendance; most automobiles sold in a day; frequency of auctions; how a dealer checks a car before buying.

An interview with a soil chemist. Experiments in which the subject is currently engaged; leading achievements during the past few years; problems he will tackle in the near future. Slant: The growing importance of soil chemistry in view of the ever-increasing demand for food from decreasing farmlands and as the population expands.

A children's museum. Founders of the museum; the number of exhibits; various features—art, ceramics, nature field trips; facts about the museum's operation; number of visitors annually.

APRIL 15

First U.S. school for deaf opens (1817) . . . Lincoln dies from wounds of previous evening (1865) . . . Titanic *sinks (1912).*

The superstition concerning $2 bills. Where does it come from? Does the mint still print these bills? Interview banks, merchants—do many people believe the deuce to be a bearer of bad luck or is it just that they mistakenly give them away as singles? Query clerks in stores to see if corners of most $2 bills are torn off in an effort to ward off ill fortune or to identify the deuce as such.

"Meter maids." Discuss the trend toward employing women as parking meter checkers. How many cities utilize women in this capacity? The first and the latest to do so. The ready—and eager—supply of woman-power for such use. Do the "meter maids" sometimes encounter hostile reaction on the part of males? Photo spread can show uniforms worn.

You think YOU have tax problems! Contrast your community's taxes with those paid in other communities, states, nations. For example, taxes in England are far worse than in U.S. Some states have no income tax, in others it is steep; commodity and sales taxes vary greatly from state to state, city to city.

APRIL 16

De Diego's Birthday in Puerto Rico . . . First play by an American produced (Royal Tyler's The Contrast, *1787, in New York) . . . Birth of Anatole France (1844) and Wilbur Wright (1867).*

Hats preferred by politicians. From derby to ten-gallon hat, a wide range of hats have been political "trademarks." Do some of the officials also believe their hats bring them good luck, as on Election Day? Is it useful for a politician to "tag" himself with a memorable lid?

A highway post office. How the rolling post office is an important factor in faster and better service; a typical route; equipment and workers. Are these mobile post offices on the increase?

Puppeteers. How the operation of a puppet show calls for all the skills and coordination needed to stage a flesh-and-blood theatrical; how the local puppeteer "pulls strings" to bring entertainment to children; plays he has written for presentation by his marionettes. How to make and where to buy puppets.

APRIL 17

Verrazano Day in New York State . . . Martin Luther excommunicated (1521) . . . Benjamin Franklin dies (1790) . . . Birth of John Pierpont Morgan (1837).

Organ repairs and remodeling. The demand for second-hand organs. Facts about the organ industry. Historic organs. How an organ is remodeled.

Special bus services. Survey the many "charter runs" of bus lines—for example, bus transportation to churches, theaters, sports events, museums, for parties and picnics. Discuss costs, advantages; show effects—the increase in Sunday school and church attendance, the number of youngsters who see a museum for the first time in this way.

A youthful wizard at checkers. Championships he or she has won; the youth's most exciting matches; checker foes who gave him the most trouble; other games in which he displays brilliance. Extend to school, state, national and international matches. Has checkers become a young man's game?

APRIL 18

Paul Revere's ride (1775) . . . San Francisco earthquake (1906) . . . James Doolittle's raid on Tokyo (1942) . . . Ernie Pyle killed (1945).

The stock of a drugstore. Compare catalogues of today's drugstore suppliers with those of fifty years ago to show how vastly different today's almost-a-department-store is from yesterday's pharmacy; nostrums that are no longer sold, changing costs of staying healthy. Other interesting sidelights: a pharmacist's rigorous training, his records of drugs sold, unusual services performed, leading non-drug items.

Adding machines. Choose one long-established company and use it to show the progress of bookkeeping—from the goose quill to today's electronic devices. Extend to show other machines and methods that have changed—contrast the earliest typewriters and today's electric models, for example. Slant: select old advertisements for office and household equipment and compare with today's mechanical marvels.

An acoustics expert at work. Methods used to achieve superior acoustics in such buildings as churches and theaters; facts about sound; what the experts say about sound problems in the average home.

APRIL 19

John Howard Payne Memorial Day . . . Patriots' Day in Maine and Massachusetts . . . Beginning of American War for Independence (Lexington and Concord, 1775) . . . End of same war, 1873 . . . Grace Kelly marries Prince Rainier III (1956).

Drum majors (and majorettes!) on parade. Many things can be done with this theme: photos of popular majorettes, learning to twirl the baton, special tricks developed by a twirler, schools for majorettes, age at which to start learning, travels of a majorette.

Living charter members of historic churches. Their vital part in religious activities. Are some of them Sunday school teachers? Highlights of the churches' history and outstanding pastors, as recalled by those members.

An extensive collection of Indian curios. Where these relics were found; how they were originally made and used; information concerning Indian life in your community (state, section of the country), as recounted by a local collector. Do Indians of today know how to make such utensils?

APRIL 20

Asser Levy first Jew in America to receive (on this day, 1657) full rights and privileges of citizenship, allowed to perform all duties . . . Birth of Adolf Hitler (1889).

Non-medical uses of X-ray machines. Show how many ways the X-ray is used in one typical city—by police to examine suspicious boxes and packages that might contain explosives; by museums to examine paintings and other objects of art; by engineers to detect unusual stresses (X-ray repair organizations will provide leads).

"When I was frightened by heights." Interview a steeplejack about his work. The highest steeples and smokestacks he has painted or repaired; safety precautions. Is he fascinated by great heights? Does he harbor any superstitions?

The wife of the local weatherman. Is she as weather-conscious as her husband? Is she the target of jokes about her husband's sometimes-fallible predictions? Does she rely on his office's forecasts when arranging trips, picnics, vacations? How do she and her husband teach their youngsters the elements of meteorology? What we should all know about weather forecasting.

APRIL 21

San Jacinto Day in Texas . . . Founding of Rome (753 B.C.) . . . Birth of Charlotte Brontë (1816) . . . Death of Mark Twain (1910) . . . Birth of Queen Elizabeth II (1926).

All in a minister's mail. Describe the pile of daily correspondence received by a typical minister: unusual requests; the average number of speaking invitations received per week; keeping in touch with former parishioners and friends; pamphlets offering items for sale to the church: money-raising efforts; letters seeking advice.

Coroners—elected or appointed? What's the situation in your city or state? Compare it with others. Describe duties of a coroner and typical training. What's the opinion of law-enforcement groups, medical associations on a coroner's training? Compare recommended and actual training. On what do people base their vote when the post is elective?

Chimney mishaps. Injuries from chimney accidents during storms, as related by brick masons. Past and present styles in chimneys; checking chimneys for safety; hints to the homeowner.

APRIL 22

Arbor Day in Nebraska . . . Oklahoma Day . . . Birth of Henry Fielding (1707) . . . Oklahoma Land Rush begins (1889).

Nationality organizations. How the clubs enable the members to keep lovely customs, songs, and traditions of their old countries alive and to make them meaningful to their youngsters today; the largest such groups and their principal activities. Possible special slants—costumes, recipes, superstitions, legends, unusual ways of celebrating holidays.

An old church cemetery. History told through inscriptions—wars, disasters, Indian raids, holocausts, epidemics. Inspiring stories of courage, sacrifice, faith can be found here.

A boat yard. Woods used; steps in the manufacture of small craft; weekly output; innovations in design and production; statistics on boating's growing popularity. Slant: How boat making is as vigorous an industry in winter as in summer.

APRIL 23

Death of Shakespeare (1616) . . . Birth of James Buchanan (1791) . . . and Stephen Douglas (1813).

Assigning house numbers. Does the city building inspector issue the numbers? The problem of working out numbers for an expanding community. Do some home builders just select numbers they like and use them? Renumbering houses when figures grow too high or are too cumbersome.

A bowling instructor's day. The common faults of beginners. Furthering the interest of boys and girls in the sport. Conducting bowling clinics. Bowling associations; the best scorers among the members; average scores; exhibitions; trick shots.

Windmills. Only a few are still operating, but many mills are preserved as museums or historic sites. The "cap," and how it was turned toward the wind; the enormously heavy stones used for grinding; the intricate, hand-hewn cogs and gears. What life for the miller was like when the mill operated daily.

APRIL 24

First publication of first regularly-issued American newspaper, Boston News-Letter *(1704) . . . Founding of Library of Congress (1800).*

The story of telephone and electric light poles. Obtaining the poles, treating and installing them. How long does the average pole last? Are car accidents or storms the primary cause of destruction? The highest poles in use; explanation of the numbers and symbols seen on poles.

The stork in odd places. Births in unusual places—cars, planes, theaters, stores. Who substituted for the doctor? How theaters and businesses prepare for the unexpected, and city statistics on such births.

Church libraries. Volunteers who serve as librarians; large church libraries and the average number of book borrowers and browsers per week or month; the most popular books; donors. And by the way—are any books not returned?

APRIL 25

First shots of U.S.-Mexican War (1846) . . . Birth of Guglielmo Marconi (1874) . . . United Nations meets for first time (San Francisco, 1945).

Barbering school. Investigate this source of old jokes: are the hoary japes justified? How long does it take to learn to give a good haircut? The instructors and the progress of the course; barbering regulations; prices charged by the school; who the clients are; earnings of barbers.

Aloft with an airline hostess. A typical day; the thrill of meeting dignitaries; her longest flight; which cities are the most attractive from the sky; her training.

School hymns. Who wrote those songs about dear old Alma Mater? Are popular college songs frequently adopted by high schools? Are they all "fighting" songs—even those at girls' schools? Do many schools have the same hymn?

APRIL 26

Confederate Memorial Day in Alabama, Florida, Georgia and Mississippi . . . Baptism of William Shakespeare (1564) . . . First British colonists land at Cape Henry (1607) . . . Birth of James Audubon (1785) . . . First lodge of Independent Order of Odd Fellows (1819).

An interview with a department store artist. Producing posters and display cards; other duties; the most effective uses of color; training required to be a commercial artist. Slant: The artist is just as effective a salesman as the clerks themselves.

Indefatigable opera fan. How frequent are his opportunities to attend the opera? His recollection of the first opera he saw; his collection of opera records; noted singers he has heard, and the foremost ones, in his judgment. How does he feel about operas in English?

Popular books at a state penitentiary. The number of books in the library and those most in demand. Are mystery or detective novels usually popular among the inmates? Is there much use of technical books by prisoners eager to prepare themselves for jobs after their release? What about legal handbooks: are there really many "jail-house lawyers"?

APRIL 27

First tariff legislation for protective purposes enacted (1816) . . . Birth of Samuel Morse (1791) and Ulysses S. Grant (1822) . . . Death of Ralph Waldo Emerson (1882).

The neon tube—how does it work? And how is it made into the bright and garish signs that flash all over America? A visit to a craftsman to show how the tubes are bent into shape. The use of a gas conductor to provide illumination.

A prominent astronomical photographer. How photography has been put to use in mapping the sky, in measuring the brightness of the stars and in determining other astronomical facts; the equipment of the subject and his best photographs; the photographer's extensive knowledge of astronomy; how his interest was awakened.

Stories of quarantine signs. The experiences of a local health officer in quarantining homes: stubborn patients; epidemic signs used by pranksters or children playing hooky from school. When *is* a home quarantined?

APRIL 28

Birth of James Monroe (1758) . . . First commercial telephone exchange opened (New Haven, 1878) . . . Execution of Benito Mussolini (1945) . . . Official end of war with Japan (1952).

Night and day at a telephone answering service. How the telephone secretaries answer calls in a client's name when he is out of the office or away from home; taking messages and orders; how the telephone company makes it possible for the service to "come in" on other lines; unusual services, messages; the "wake-up" service.

The local building inspector. He's responsible for safety at the neighborhood level, and his knowledge can prevent disaster at the reader's home. How he examines houses to eliminate fire and other hazards; the most common faults found by the inspector; how he'd inspect a new residence if he were considering buying it.

Gourds. The growing popularity of natural gourds —used for decorative purposes, as water dippers, as homes for martin birds, as musical instruments. "Do-it-yourself" information on this age-old gift of nature, and painting techniques.

APRIL 29

Lincoln University (first Negro university) incorporated (1854) . . . Zipper patented by Gideon Sundback (1913).

A farmer who is an aviation enthusiast. How the airplane serves functional purposes down on the farm; ways in which the businessman-farmer makes use of his aircraft—locating stray animals, visiting buyers at terminal centers, dusting crops; costs; time saved; emergency use of craft. Is his wife a flying "bug"? What about his children?

An unusual Boy Scout family in your city. What local family has the largest number of members of the Boy Scouts? The Scout activities of these members; how they use their skills and knowledge at home; awards received, badges won; one day's "good deeds" recounted.

Boats on parade. Where to go—and when—to see boats of yesterday and today: whale boats, atom-powered craft, a regatta, Indian canoes, clipper ships, and so on. Illustrate with photographs, or use as the basis of a quiz.

APRIL 30

George Washington takes oath of office (1789) . . . Louisiana Purchase (1803) . . . Hitler commits suicide (1945).

Portrait of a cub scout den mother. Use your tape-recorder (and camera) to depict the fun and confusion of a den mother's job—the questions she must answer, the decisions, the chatter, the discipline. The "mother" provides the slant: her personality, where she takes the cubs.

Grateful ex-prisoners. Letters the chief of police and the sheriff have received from former convicts who give major credit to law officials for their rehabilitation since release; acts of kindness and fatherly advice that caused the prisoners to "see the light."

The art "explosion." In many communities, painting and sketching form the leading hobby: demonstrate by showing growth of a state art association, as related by its president. Profile the classes available to young and old—with photos of exhibits and prize-winning works. Sidelights show how business and professional leaders, housewives and teen-agers, have taken up painting as a hobby.

MAY 1

May Day . . . First penny postal cards go on sale (1783) . . . Commander Dewey sails into Manila Bay, destroys Spanish fleet (1898).

Frightened? Interview a physician and psychologist to describe what happens when people are terrified: how adrenal glands work, effect on pulse, breathing, etc. Are old superstitions true—can hair "stand on end" or "turn white"?

Greenhouse at home. The garden club can put you in touch with women who cultivate orchids, African violets, and other rare flowers at home—on window sills or in portable nurseries. Slant: Their homes are filled with Spring all year long.

Air purification. Civic and industrial groups are battling contamination of air from factories, cars, industrial plants, furnaces. Is this a threat in your town (city, state)? What groups are active in the effort? What do physicians say of dangers of air pollution?

MAY 2

Death of Leonardo da Vinci (1519) . . . Hudson Bay Company chartered (1670) . . . First radio facsimile transmission across Atlantic (New York to London—a drawing —1920).

Almanacs. A collection of old almanacs can set you off on several stories—the books themselves, the "hints" for the housewife and farmer, the collector, the jokes and light sayings, the illustrations—compare these in different almanacs. Extension service agents and rare book dealers can generally lead you to almanac collectors.

Rainy day entertaining. Ask teachers, scout leaders, camp counselors, recreational facility directors for a list of ideas to keep tots and pre-schoolers happy and busy at home on wet or nasty days, or get a similar list from members of a women's group. If the ideas are "tested," so much the better.

Animal intelligence. A good veterinarian can supply surprising facts on the IQ's of popular pets and domestic animals, with anecdotes from pet owners, farmers, stable owners, pet shop personnel.

MAY 3

First medical college established (Philadelphia, 1765) . . . Birth of Jacob A. Riis (1849) . . . Third Sunday in May proclaimed "I Am An American Day" (1940).

What you pay for. . . . The citizen's *pro rata* cost of such municipal, state, or national government activities as education, sanitation, crime and its prevention. On latter subject, for example, you could figure at local level the salaries paid to the police department, court personnel, prison expenses, etc.

An interview with a society photographer. The knack of "shooting" society pictures: difficult assignments; taking wedding photos; notable parties the subject has photographed.

Radio and television stations as finders. Slant: How the stations, by finding lost persons and pets via broadcasts, serve as unofficial missing persons bureaus. Average number of appeals per month; the most unusual cases; making certain the requests are authentic and not practical jokes. Do more girls run away than boys?

MAY 4

Rhode Island Independence Day . . . Peter Minuit lands on Manhattan Island (1626) . . . Birth of Horace Mann (1796) . . . Haymarket Square Riot (Chicago, 1886).

The woman's press club in your state. The dean of the members; profiles of the officials and their jobs; chief objectives of the organization; "scoops" of feminine stars in journalism.

Fossils in your own back yard? University anthropologists can explain what remnants of earlier cultures can be found in your community (state, region). Indian artifacts abound; indeed (story slant) many people do a thriving business in sales of arrowheads and Indian implements. Another slant: many high school and college clubs are devoted to such collecting.

Memories of a magistrate. Reflections by a jurist on his constant efforts to bring about settlements of family quarrels; his views on the causes and cures of husband-wife problems, and unusual methods he has used to resolve such difficulties.

MAY 5

Death of Napoleon Bonaparte (1821) . . . Founding of the American Medical Association (1847).

Can you pass your kids' tests? At a local school, obtain sample questions from tests given to children in the third grade and up—covering such subjects as history, arithmetic, geography, space. Ask the readers to see how well they'd do against the average children's scores.

Unusual church bulletin boards. A collection of the "bulletin board barbs" that have appeared—such as the message, "What is missing from ch—ch? UR!" Similar sayings, humorous and serious, that have attracted wide attention. Slant: Photo feature.

A woman watch repairer. How she acquired her skills and interest; learning the trade. Does the average person put as much trust in a woman repairer as in a male? Oldest watches the subject has repaired.

MAY 6

Founding of the American Bible Association (1816) . . . Birth of Sigmund Freud (1856) and Robert E. Peary (1856) . . . Eiffel Tower opens (1889) . . . Hindenburg *dirigible disaster (1937) . . . Corregidor surrenders to Japan (1942).*

Strike settler. Interview an arbitrator who works with industry and labor. What are his techniques for restoring calm, bringing about orderly discussion, reconciling differences? Does he practice these techniques in his everyday life? Strikes he has settled or prevented; arduous efforts; other applications of arbitration procedures.

Fun by the numbers. Mathematics teachers can supply you with puzzles involving arithmetic and simple mathematics. A growing hobby, with many clubs (in high schools and colleges particularly), devoted to fooling around with figures.

Mechanical banks and toys. Put a penny in here—and the mechanical banks of the late 19th century flip it through the air and deposit it there. Show collection of local hobbyist (often bank officials). Antique stores can supply antique toys for photographic spread on Grandpa's boyhood playthings.

MAY 7

Birth of Robert Browning (1812) and the composers Johannes Brahms (1833) and Peter Illyitch Tschaikovsky (1840) . . . Sinking of the Lusitania *(1915) . . . Germany surrenders (1945).*

Out of gas. Interview operators of local service stations about their most unusual experiences in responding to SOS calls for gas: longest distances; deadbeats; attempts at robbery by persons faking empty gas tanks. What day of the week leads in the number of "out of gas" customers? What is the standard excuse of the embarrassed customer? Do more women than men get in this pickle?

Weather watching. How to forecast the weather by cloud formations; various types of clouds; which clouds can be "seeded" to produce rain; other weather tips provided by the skies—a halo around the moon, red sun, etc. Check superstitions with a local weather expert.

Color blindness. This relatively common eye disorder is now most often diagnosed at the elementary school level. What does it mean to the child who is color blind? How did he get that way? What careers are barred to him? Percentage of people so handicapped.

MAY 8

Hernando de Soto discovers the Mississippi (1541)... Birth of Harry S. Truman (1884).

Stories about bondsmen. Unusual offers as security —jewelry, stamp collections, real estate; uneasy moments for bondsmen; what the reader should do if he ever requires a bond posted for him; charges for the service; regulations for protection of the public.

Domes. Extraordinary ones; the oldest; unique clocks in domes; the construction of a vast dome as described by an architect; historic domes around the country and world.

"Coin collectors" who are coin collectors. Bankers, cashiers and others who are also numismatists: the value of their collections; how and where most valuable coins were obtained.

MAY 9

First U.S. Protestant Episcopal Church established (Jamestown, 1607) . . . Birth of John Brown (1800) and Sir James Barrie (1860).

Trailer courts. Auto courts, like roadside cabins and bowling alleys, have grown respectable and lavish since the end of World War II. Show modern facilities and luxuries available to nomads of the highway; discuss network of courts; prices; typical residents; anecdotes of proprietors and trailer families.

After you "junk" your car. What happens to the car after you sell it? Export sales; stripping of the car for useful parts; how the steel of the body is used again; markets abroad and at home for special vehicles (New York's Fifth Avenue buses go to South America . . . old convertibles to India for taxis . . . hot-rodders are a market . . . all proving there's life in the old buggy yet!).

Hypnotism. Is it used by any local dentists, doctors or at hospitals? Dangers of amateur hypnosis; predictions by local medical authorities on its possible usefulness in operations, childbirth; profile of an outstanding practitioner.

MAY 10

Confederate Memorial Day in North Carolina and South Carolina . . . Astor Place Riots in New York (over theatrical performances, 1849) . . . Death of Thomas ("Stonewall") Jackson (1863) . . . Transcontinental railroad completed (1869).

Bait. Sometimes it seems that every fisherman has a different philosophy and set of rules about the inducement at the end of the hook. Obtain statements, hints, techniques from one group—all the anglers at one pond, lake or stream, for example, or members of the same club—and compare them. Do they agree at all? Special tricks of fly-tying. What does the game warden think of all this? Does Junior's worm often succeed where costly devices fail?

Jam and jelly time. Because the younger generation buys these delicacies, it's time for some kitchen expert to reveal her at-home step-by-step secrets. Additional data: give information on berry-picking—which berries are edible, which poisonous.

Sheriffs and ten-gallon hats. Do many sheriffs go in for broad-brimmed, ten-gallon hats? Or for other picturesque apparel? What the average sheriff of today wears.

MAY 11

Birth of John "Johnny Appleseed" Chapman (1768) and Irving Berlin (1888).

Pageants. How children in their schools and churches and adults in municipal functions keep the pageant alive and growing. Describe seasonal, regional pageants; interview professionals who travel from city to city, staging the same pageant again and again, with ever-changing casts; industrial pageants and roadshows.

A publicity director for a college. His duties; the importance of photographs; unusual stunts staged by the director that reaped wide publicity; stirring up interest in college events, from football games to scholastic achievements.

Profile of a veteran window washer. The task of keeping the display windows of local stores clean. How often are they washed? Cleaning the windows of high apartment houses and skyscrapers—how these workers become accustomed to great heights; accidents; acts of heroism. P.S.—What *do* they see through those windows as they wash?

MAY 12

Birth of Florence Nightingale (1820) . . .
American Tract Society organized (1825).

Chess pieces. Pictures of rare pieces in local personal or museum collections. How the various pieces evolved to present designs. Rare sets picked up at auctions and in antique shops. Chess in our day-to-day language—"pawns," "checkmate."

How to read a blueprint. Explaining the complex building trade's blueprints to laymen—with explanations from construction experts, draftsmen, electricians, and with special attention to symbols. How blueprints are made, from start to finish.

Arm in a sling? There's more to broken bones than the layman knows—explain simple and compound fractures as described by a physician. First aid. New developments in bone surgery. How people feel about casts—the autographs, "coming out" parties. Physiotherapy for healing fractures.

MAY 13

First practical American printing press patented (Samuel Rust, 1821) . . . U.S. Navy nurses' corps authorized (1908) . . . Birth of Joe Louis (1914).

He knows the price of everything! An interview with an appraiser, whose range of knowledge often extends from antiques to modern art, from mechanical equipment to jewelry. Husband-and-wife teams; specialized appraisers in technical fields; the insurance company appraiser. How appraisers are paid, trained; unusual assignments abroad.

Migrating birds. Are you on one of the "paths" chosen by migrating birds? (Note: butterflies and moths also migrate over vast distances.) Discuss these instinctive voyages; bird sanctuaries; bird banding; the dangers birds face from natural elements, hunters, blinding rays of searchlights; the dangers they present to airplanes.

A motorcycle club. The activities of the club in motorcycle polo, local races, hare and hound chases, turkey runs, "secret destination" rides, and economy runs. Emphasis on law-abiding, sports-minded, skilled membership.

MAY 14

Vaccination discovered by Edward Jenner (1796) . . . Lewis and Clark begin their expedition (1804) . . . Patent granted Gail Borden for commercial condensed milk (1851).

Welcome mat at the army camp. The services have "open house" at least once a year, frequently more often. Where should tourists in your city (state, region) go to see the armed services at work and in training? Camps, bases, ports; particularly impressive displays (as of rockets, jets, subs); what the kids should be sure to see.

Star-gazers. Once a hobby for the few, astronomy is now enjoying vast popularity among all ages. Build story around: youth groups, a particular observatory, "do-it-yourself" telescopes, seasonal "displays" in the skies, satellite-watching system, astronomy for amateur navigators, sky-watchers at a local airport, famed local astronomer.

Photography and a local chamber of commerce. Making the best use of pictures to "sell" the advantages of county, city or state to industry and tourists; pictorial brochures, motion pictures and slide presentations.

MAY 15

Straw Hat Day . . . Founding of National Woman Suffrage Association (1869) . . . First regular airmail service (1918).

Hey, taxi! Little-known facts about our familiar cabs: local, city, state laws—differences in cost-per-mile in various cities; meters versus the "zone system"; jitneys; the cab-driver's own secret language (a non-tipper can be a "stiff," $5.00 is called a "pound"); mileage clocked by typical drivers; maintenance of cabs used on three shifts daily.

Codes used by kids. Check in a few schools and camps, and you'll find that youngsters have written and verbal codes of their own, from the familiar "pig Latin" to involved cryptograms. Can the reader "break" their typical messages?

Straw hat time. The steps in the manufacture of the traditional skimmers and the new styles of straws. Hand labor involved abroad. Favorite straw hats from the Twenties still proudly worn.

MAY 16

First American colonist (Jacob Leisler) hanged for treason (New York, 1691) . . . First state Fish Commission authorized (Massachusetts, 1856) . . . First U.S. nickels issued (1866).

Here come the tourists! With vacation season just a few weeks away, individuals and cities are now preparing for the annual invasion—or, at least, are doing their best to lure travelers. What are the people in one particular village (city, state, region) doing to make this year a better one for all?

Camera historians. How state and local historical societies document their activities with still and motion-picture cameras. For example—photos of old homes, antique furniture, farm implements, interesting local customs, unusual gardens, distinguished visitors.

Our daily bread. The story of a loaf of bread: favorite recipes for unusual local breads and rolls; how a modern bakery packages and delivers its wares; what happens to unsold loaves; bread additives, pro and con; bread recipes from foreign restaurants and fraternal groups; has calorie-consciousness affected sales?

MAY 17

Birth of Edward Jenner (1749) . . . First "Kentucky Derby" (1814) . . . U.S. Supreme Court desegregation decision (1954).

Let's explore a cave. Caverns and caves are found in abundance in America, and spelunking has become a booming hobby. Join a group of young spelunkers as they descend. Safety precautions; interesting discoveries; scientific values. Survey local (regional, national) caves that may be explored.

What are the odds? Interview statisticians, actuaries, card experts, safety engineers to present an overall picture of the odds one faces—in games, travels, health, business. Tie in with specific subjects: an automobile trip (odds that tires will go flat); Friday the 13th; hospitalization; perfect bridge hands; a hole in one in a golf tourney.

Charities. The fake appeals to guard against; deductions on income tax for charitable contributions explained; where the city's (state's) charity dollar goes. What charitable organizations do with your old clothes, furniture, toys, books; bargains at charity thrift shops; new wrinkles in local money-raising efforts. A tireless worker for a worthy charity.

MAY 18

First accredited colonial election held (Massachusetts, 1631) to elect Governor (John Winthrop) . . . Halley's Comet passes over the sun (1910).

Our fantastic credit system. Show the multitudinous aspects of credit in one community. What happens to the check you write; clearing houses, exchanges; the credit clubs; how installment houses check your credit rating.

Staffs of local churches. Behind the pastors are a number of persons devoting a great deal of time to church operations: secretaries to the ministers, the musical directors, recreational leaders, volunteer teachers, and so on.

A veteran college boxing coach. Was he a fighter himself? His record as a boxing coach; champions he has trained; his favorites in professional pugilism; step-by-step development of a boxer.

MAY 19

Anne Boleyn beheaded (1536) . . . Death of William Bradford (1657) . . . A national game law is approved (1796) . . . Patent granted for electric fire alarm system (1857).

Is there anything we can't rent? In big cities and in many small ones, you can now rent anything from electrical appliances to nursery furniture. Survey your area to show the astonishing number of objects that can be rented by the average family—mink coats, cars, a yacht, a plane. Slant: new services for the homeowner.

They grow their own spices. Housewives who grow herbs and prepare their own spices and condiments. How to start your own herb garden, on your window or just outside the kitchen door. Favorite recipes of homemakers employing these home-grown delights.

Contempt of court. Ask a judge to explain the numerous ways in which a person can be in "contempt of court." Origin of term; famous cases; the range of penalties that may be imposed. Tie in with any recent case. (A local Legal Aid Society can provide valuable information.)

MAY 20

Death of Christopher Columbus (1506) . . . Birth of Honoré Balzac (1799) . . . Lindbergh begins first solo flight across Atlantic (1927).

Livestock king of your county. The leading breed; improving the stock; the size of the ranch; number of workers; marketing methods and problems; controlling diseases. Is his story a rags-to-riches saga?

Train whistles. A behind-the-scenes interview with a veteran railroad engineer of your county—the meanings of the different whistles.

A cracker plant. How the crackers are made; the amount of materials used daily, and the output per day; cleanliness measures at the plant. Changing tastes in crackers—are they sweeter, filled with more ingredients, enriched with vitamins?

MAY 21

First bicycle in U.S. (New York, 1819) . . . First Democratic National Convention (Baltimore, 1832) . . . Founding of the American Red Cross (1881) . . . Lindbergh lands at Le Bourget airport, Paris, after 33½ hour flight (1927).

National Maritime Day. May is the month that made history in Atlantic Ocean transportation. The *Savannah,* the first steamship to cross the Atlantic using steam power, sailed from Savannah, Georgia, in May, 1819, and Charles A. Lindbergh landed in Paris on May 21, 1927. Comments by county or state historians.

Latest twists in amusement rides. There's always something new, something different at amusement parks. Designers of new rides; the most popular rides, both old and new, how rides are transported from one community to the next; safety measures at the amusement park. (Most amusement parks open in May.)

Booking agents. For lectures, concerts, cabaret managers and others, the booking agent is the indispensable man. How does he find and "sell" talent? The task of mapping a schedule. Has the booking agent been an entertainer himself? Who uses his services?

MAY 22

National Maritime Day . . . Empire Day in Canada . . . Birth of Richard Wagner (1813) and Sir Arthur Conan Doyle (1859).

"Fatties." What local physicians, teachers, psychiatrists say about the fat child. The dangers of childhood obesity, psychologically and physically. Eating habits and how to correct them.

Flower fables. List and discuss our superstitions and traditional sayings about flowers, from "She loves me, she loves me not" to the reflection of a buttercup on one's chin.

Date etiquette, sorority-style. Quiz the girls at a college sorority about their rules with their dates, their special slang and colloquialisms, favorite ways to spend the evening; conclude with quotation from a veteran housemother on whether "date etiquette" has really changed over the years.

MAY 23

Captain Kidd hanged in London (1701) . . . Benjamin Franklin invents bifocal eyeglasses (1785) . . . Birth of Margaret Fuller (1810).

The public debt—city, state and federal. We hear about the "public debt," but what does it mean to us and to future generations? Our share of the public debt, per capita. Comments from politicians, economists, bankers and the "man-in-the-street."

Oldest dance teacher in your city in length of career. His estimate of number of students; former pupils who have made quite a dancing name for themselves; dance crazes of bygone years; the activities of a dance teaching society. Does the teacher plan to retire soon?

Aviation club of a college. How was it started? An interview with the president. The instructors; facts about the organization; the club's planes; longest flights; members who have logged the most hours; members from "flying families." Any girls in the membership?

MAY 24

Peter Minuit buys Manhattan for $24 (1626) . . . Brooklyn Bridge opens (1883).

Minor or adult? Drawing the line and making the quick guess—as related by theater cashiers, bus drivers, railroad conductors, ticket sellers at sports events, and bartenders. Staunch denials on the part of youngsters. Describe regulations and penalties.

Wheel chairs and crutches. Survey of the many local organizations and churches that furnish the sick with wheel chairs and other aids. Other services for the temporarily or permanently handicapped.

Mottoes and quotations adorning executives' walls. The new twists given to old sayings. For example, one mayor altered a sign in his office from "A word to the wise is sufficient" to "A word from the wise is sufficient."

MAY 25

Birth of Ralph Waldo Emerson (1803) . . . First American troops in France arrive at Rouen (1917).

Parking problems. Schools, churches, hospitals, and other public institutions are now faced with parking and traffic problems. What are zoning regulations? How do architects and planners estimate likely traffic loads? How does "downtown" congestion affect long-range plans?

Street musicians. Interview a "street band" or such sidewalk entertainers as an organ-grinder, blind violinist, or "one-man band." How and when did the musicians learn their trades? What are the differences in their income from neighborhood to neighborhood? Any touching experiences with children? Average "donations."

Absenteeism. Choose a typical day in a typical community for a survey of absences at all levels—school, business, industry, government. What are primary causes, excuses, preventatives? Income and man-hours lost. Is "blue Monday" the worst day of the week?

MAY 26

Kansas-Nebraska Act passed (1854) . . . Birth of Al Jolson (1886) . . . Smallpox epidemic sweeps Boston (1721).

Scales, large and small. The largest in local use, in contrast with the tiny scales and balances employed in laboratories. Information dealing with all types of scales, including platform scales, those in grocery stores, and weighing machines that furnish weight-and-fortune cards for the penny-droppers. Government checking of scales.

An insight into a forestry experiment station. Slant: Constant efforts to make the forest a better servant of mankind. Scientific forestry as practiced by the nation's Forest Service. Latest experiments and the results so far.

Congressmen of your state as fishermen and hunters. Where they prefer to try their ability—and luck. Their greatest moments of success as Izaak Waltons and Nimrods. Do their wives accompany them and do well themselves?

MAY 27

Achsah Young executed for witchcraft (1647) in Massachusetts . . . Birth of Amelia Bloomer (1818) and Julia Ward Howe (1819).

The most prolific inventor in your state. The number of patents to his credit; the best-known of his creations; his latest invention. Has he enjoyed considerable earnings from his devices? His laboratory. The timetable of the creation of one invention.

The youngest circuit judge in your state. His legal career; the most colorful trials at which he has presided; his opinions on the prevention of crime and the rehabilitation of criminals; highspots in the history of circuit-riding, as he recalls them.

"How I met my husband." Interview wives of local ministers on this subject. What do they think about love at first sight? Their recommendations for a successful marriage. Does the public expect too much of a parson's wife? Couples who have resided in the largest number of places.

MAY 28

First color "talkie" released (On With the Show, *1929*) . . . *Birth of Dionne quintuplets (1934)* . . . *Dunkirk evacuation (1940).*

"Lost and found" departments. How many in a typical community? Consider just a few—at stores, police stations, restaurants, parks, terminals, movie houses. Do many lost objects remain unclaimed? Where do we lose most things—and when? What are some of the huge and unlikely possessions lost?

Maintaining a city sewer system. Little-known facts, common troubles, unstopping sewer lines; children or pets who venture into street drains; new developments in pipes. Costs in cities large and small.

Strange municipal laws. Old-time statutes never repealed—one city has a law against disturbing neighbors by snoring! Look through the local city code.

MAY 29

Constantinople captured by Turks (1453) . . . Birth of Patrick Henry (1736) . . . Constitution ratified by 13th State (Rhode Island, 1790) . . . Edmond Hillary reaches top of Mt. Everest (1953).

A woman department store owner. Her start in the mercantile business; why she entered such work; the number of women employed in the store; the owner's business philosophy.

Pets in unusual places—shopping centers, schools, firehouses, roundhouses. Do the animals belong to individuals, or are they neighborhood pets? Tricks performed by the pets to earn their keep. Do any act as sentinels? Odd pets—talking parrots, tame "wild" animals, small and large pets.

The latest in trick photography. Amusing trick effects achieved by members of a camera club in your city or county. Combining different pictures; "putting" a person in a bottle or pitcher; the members' own greeting cards, announcements of birth of children, etc.

MAY 30

Memorial Day . . . Confederate Memorial Day in Virginia . . . Joan of Arc burned at stake (1431) . . . Patent granted for ice-cream freezer (1848).

Keyboard criminology. Typewriter comparisons made by such law officers as FBI agents. How each typewriter is as individual as a person's handwriting; show examples of "personality" of individual machines; outstanding instances of identification by typewriting; forgery by means of adding to a typewritten account.

Newspaper jargon. An editor's explanation of a multitude of expressions—"flash," "sob sister," "beat," "cub," "legman," "morgue," "printer's devil," "lead," "stick," "hell-box," "hatchet man," "rim," etc. Discuss pranks played upon neophytes.

The decline of the milking stool. Consult the Extension Service in your state about the number of milking machines in use today as compared to a decade ago. How much time is devoted to milking at a large dairy? Slant: The increase in milk production within recent years is a step forward in meeting the table requirements of a growing population. But is the public buying as much milk as formerly?

MAY 31

Birth of Walt Whitman (1819) . . . Johnstown (Pa.) flood, 2,200 die (1889) . . . First taxis, New York (1907) . . . Battle of Jutland (1916).

The business side of a small airport. The various members of the office force, including the bookkeepers. Are any of the office workers aviators? How many shifts are needed? Upkeep of field and facilities; safety precautions; links with other fields and military services.

Woes of a program chairman. The tasks of booking speakers; prevailing upon notables to appear; celebrities who have traveled great distances to address the organizations. Program changes at the last minute; fees to lecturers; offering hospitality to guests.

Could you be a professional typist? Many people consider typing a good source of part-time income. Interview a public stenographer to get her advice. Which trades give her the most business? Discuss typing manuscripts for writers; charges, skills needed. Does the typist regularly handle monthly statements for merchants, physicians, and dentists? How many words or pages per hour? What are most demanding assignments? How does one get started?

JUNE 1

Birth of Brigham Young (1801) . . . "Don't give up the ship" uttered by Captain James Lawrence (1813) . . . Army Signal Corps established (1860).

Somnambulism. Remarkable cases of sleepwalking; instances in which somnambulists have performed feats that they would not have dared otherwise. What causes sleepwalking? What should be done about it?

Escape artist. Profile of a magician who manages to make his escape from handcuffs, locked trunks, vaults, jails. The time required for his escapes. His physical training, practice. Has he ever failed?

Convention city. A special view of a city that is the scene of a large number of conventions. The busiest months; income to the community; how the Chamber of Commerce helps in formulation of arrangements; pleasures for the visiting organizations; problems of visitors.

JUNE 2

Birth of Thomas Hardy (1840) . . . First night baseball game (Fort Wayne, 1883) . . . Queen Elizabeth II crowned (1953).

Doctors as musicians. How musical activities provide moments of relaxation for the rushed M.D. Music as therapy. Members of the medical profession who belong to orchestras; a physician who can play several musical instruments.

Old-fashioned dishes. Old-time foods that still hold great appeal for the oldest residents of your county; the recipes. Note: keep alert for special holiday dishes for future articles—i.e., popcorn balls for Christmas trees, "remedies" for spring fever.

Trapping gun smugglers. How guards at a state penitentiary detect guns and such other metal items as hack saws and knives carried secretly by visitors to the institution. The latest in gun-detectors; how such devices prevent prison breaks. What are other, less obvious items commonly smuggled into jails—food? candy? narcotics?

JUNE 3

Confederate Memorial Day in Kentucky, Louisiana, Tennessee and Texas . . . Memorial Day in Arkansas . . . Birth of Jefferson Davis (1808) . . . Death of Stephen Douglas (1861).

A farm that has been owned and tilled by the same family for a century or longer. The size of the farm; the price of the land at the time of the purchase; the original owner of the tract and his heirs who still own the property; the ancient homestead and antiques in it; the productivity of the acres and records in production.

The constant fight against rabies. The work of the ASPCA and city and county health departments in this respect. Animals other than dogs that carry the disease; progress in treatment and prevention; ways in which a community mobilizes against rabies, such as rallying to find a person bitten by a rabid animal.

Silhouettes of the famous. The readers are challenged to identify these silhouettes, turned out by a local silhouette artist. The normal time for cutting a silhouette. Subjects can be local, regional, national.

JUNE 4

First double-decked steamboat launched (Wheeling, West Virginia, 1816) . . . Battle of Midway begins (1942).

Wedding decorations. The work that goes into the decorating for an average wedding; specialists in the field; lavish weddings; rush months; what happens to the decorations.

Old mines that are now inactive. Why activities there were suspended. Is there reason to believe that work will be resumed at some of these mines? Who operated them? Safety measures when mines close down; "bootlegging" from inactive mines.

Resignations of governors within your state's annals. The reasons; the governors' successors; subsequent events in the lives of chief executives who resigned.

JUNE 5

First safe deposit vault opens for business (New York, 1865).

A woman "country doctor." What led her to devote her life to this aspect of medical practice? Her education; the beginnings of her practice, and her first patients. Her rules for good health.

Folk songs of your state. Build your story around a singer or musician who has collected a large number of songs on tape or record. How the old tunes are kept alive in rural areas; what they tell us about history, manners, customs, daily life of other days.

Hunting decoys. Do any local hunters still whittle their own? How to make and rig decoys; the big market for antique duck decoys in antique stores; tricks of the trade in duck blinds.

JUNE 6

Birth of Nathan Hale (1755) . . . First drive-in movie opens (Camden, N.J., 1933) . . . D-Day (1944).

Save the bones! Question waitresses and restaurateurs about requests they receive to save bones or scraps for Fido. Describe elaborate lengths some restaurants go to in this regard—special little bags, with messages imprinted, in which these delicacies can be carried home. Publicity and good-will value of such little extras.

Color in your life. What designers, decorators, psychologists and advertisers know about color and you. Colors that make people buy . . . work harder . . . look better . . . feel more "at home" in public places . . . recover faster from illnesses. Slants: color in the schoolroom, factory, hospital.

An interview with a "Good Humor" man. What do these bell-ringing ice-cream salesmen on bicycles or in trucks do during the winter months? Their conversations with kids; changing tastes. Do kids ask for credit? Must salesmen ever baby-sit? Unusual experiences. Vastness of industry.

JUNE 7

Death of Mohammed (632) . . . Patent granted for automatic electric block, railroads (1870) . . . Death of Edwin Booth (1893).

"Twins in names" in your city. Instances of such confusion, as mix-ups in mail and telephone calls. Are some of the "twins" close friends? Do any look alike? Political confusion with names—there are several John F. Kennedys now in politics, some of them Republicans.

Income sources for shut-ins. Base your story on actual people and their activities. Do any operate a magazine subscription service? Other telephone selling; clipping services; specialty cooking; preparation of mailing lists; collection letters and calls. Show income received, costs of operation.

An insight into the office of a county supervisor. His various duties and those he deems the most interesting. Issuing orders for purchases; the largest orders. The supervisor's assistants.

JUNE 8

Birth of Frank Lloyd Wright (1869) . . . Patenting of first vacuum cleaner (1869) . . . Postal cards authorized (1872).

Child labor laws. Before summer and other vacation periods, it's good to remind youngsters and employers of laws governing youth work, hours, conditions, wages, and so on. Contrast with laws thirty or fifty years ago, as described by civic officials, oldsters who went to work early in their lives, and health experts.

Night-shift workers. Portraits of the men and women who work while the rest of the community snores. How do their jobs affect their leisure, shopping, sleeping habits? Family life of a night worker.

Yesterday's cooking utensils. Pictures (from a historical society) of tools and cooking aids from pioneer days for modern housewives to try to identify. Slant: Today's cooks would be lost in yesterday's kitchens!

JUNE 9

Birth of John Howard Payne ("Home Sweet Home") in 1791 . . . Tax withholding authorized by Congress (1943).

Flowers in the hospital. Interview local nurses about their experiences (both pleasant and unpleasant) with flowers. For example, what about allergic reactions—the patients' and their own? Their tricks and suggestions on keeping flowers fresh. Any superstitions? Favorite flowers of patients? What's done with vases, bowls and baskets in which the flowers arrived? Largest, oddest bouquets ever sent.

The last of the ferries. Those still in operation in your state or region, and the extent of their use; a veteran ferryman and his memories. Slant: The part played by ferries in the state's transportation system before the advent of modern highway systems, bridges and tunnels.

A librarian who has turned to writing. Magazines that have published her short stories or articles; her own literary tastes; famous authors she has met; how her experience in a library has helped her as an author.

JUNE 10

Wilkes expedition to explore South Seas (first fitted out by U.S. government) returns to New York after almost four years (1842).

Unusual "dividing line" signs between counties. Signs that proclaim merits, in Chamber of Commerce style; interesting claims; signs with odd shapes or lettering; competitive announcements by neighbors.

A prominent entomologist. The cataloguing of the many different species of insects in section, state or country. The job of collecting insects for identification, and the roles played by hobbyists, commercial collectors, museums, colleges; the state's most harmful insect; how insects adjust to DDT and other insecticides; the "wars" between insects and how nature keeps the species in balance.

A collector of old phonograph records. The oldest records in his collection; how and where acquired; at what cost. Slant: How these records constitute a history of the nation's changing tastes. Record clubs and correspondence. Is his collection ever used (and if so, how) by schools, organizations, radio or TV stations?

JUNE 11

Kamehameha Day in Hawaii . . . Birth of Richard Strauss (1864).

On tour with an orchestra. "One-night stands," at home or abroad, present innumerable special problems—from matters of food and laundry to recreation. Show how these experienced travelers cope with such obstacles; how they pack; how they compress their sightseeing. Do they have travel tips for the traveling family?

Superstitions on the job. From theater to retailing, many professions have their own superstitions and rituals: actors won't whistle backstage; some pilots refuse to be photographed before a flight. Check into other examples of traditional hexes and jinxes one encounters in various trades and enterprises.

Tower adventures. The men who climb towers of radio and television stations. Their highest climbs; mishaps or near accidents. Does height ever frighten the climbers?

JUNE 12

First naval battle of the Revolution (1775) . . . Patent for gas mask granted (1849) . . . Senate passes bill for direct election of Senators (1912).

A personality in a college choir. The American student is apparently the "singing-est" in the world. Build a photo-illustrated story about a new girl in a college choir: how she is chosen; the director; rehearsals; tours; most popular songs. Extend with facts about "choir exchanges" between countries, associations in field, famous alumni.

The cost of being a cop. Clothes help to make a policeman—but may also keep him broke. Look into the matter of his uniforms, and the costs; see what he buys, what he's supplied. How long does a uniform last? How about comfort? Find out why many officers must pay for the bullets for their guns; the cost of the policeman's shoes, and who pays for new soles and heels (yes—for the most part, Officer O'Rourke does!)

A college gymnastic team. The amazing stunts performed by these undergraduate acrobats; wire-walking and trapeze routines; their rigid training and health regimens. A photo feature.

JUNE 13

Rhode Island passes act against importation of slaves (1774) . . . Birth of Winfield Scott (1786) . . . Birth of William Butler Yeats (1865).

A day with a hotel doorman. Handling luggage may be the smallest part of his job. The odd services he's asked to perform; meeting celebrities; parking cars; unusual tips. How it feels to stand there and "watch the world go by."

An interview with a ring physician. His recollections of the most exciting matches he has watched; boxers who have taken unusual punishment; his comments on how long you and I—average folk—could last in the ring with a fighter; common ring injuries; how he goes about checking a fighter.

An interview with a landscape architect. Landscape architecture fulfills two needs—beauty and usefulness. How cities employ such architects to create or improve parks, gardens, recreation areas. Camouflaging sore spots; what the home-owner should know about landscaping.

JUNE 14

Flag Day . . . Founding of the U.S. Army (1775) . . . Stars and Stripes becomes national flag (1777) . . . Birth of Harriet Beecher Stowe (1811) and Robert Marion LaFollette (1855) . . . Germans enter Paris (1940).

Boarding house hash! Is it becoming a thing of the past? Ask veteran operators of your city. Does old-time cooking appeal to the patrons most of all? Are boarding houses on the decline?

Health laws in industry. Improvement of working conditions through legislation; safety devices; water supplies and sanitation methods. Slant: How meeting higher standards in lighting, ventilation and space assures better production as well as better health.

Flag Day. Battle flags in the museums of your state: battles in which they were carried; how they have been preserved.

JUNE 15

Signing of Magna Carta (1215) . . . Benjamin Franklin's kite-flying experiment (1752) . . . General Slocum *disaster in New York (1904).*

Pre-natal clinics. Activities in this field—including lectures and motion pictures helpful to expectant mothers and nervous husbands. Such instruction relieves busy doctors from much of the time consumed in teaching mothers the practical side of child nursing. Picture sequence: "expectant father" learns how to bathe an infant, using a rubber doll as the victim.

Restoring eyesight. Interview a leading eye specialist of your state. Successful operations for the return of eyesight; reactions of the subjects when eyesight is regained; "eye banks."

Keeping track of trays at drive-in restaurants. Average losses in a month; offers of rewards in tray thefts. Are teen-agers actually the worst offenders? Practical jokes by customers.

JUNE 16

Ancient Arabic Order of Nobles of the Mystic Shrine established (New York, 1871).

Songs of railroad men. Is "Casey Jones" the most popular among the train clan of your county? Look into triumphs and tragedies that inspired songs; railroad workers who have a reputation as musicians.

How not to scare children. Methods used by doctors, dentists, barbers, nurses, and others to maintain or produce calmness in the boys and girls with whom they work, and what the parent can learn from their long experience. Is most fear in the anticipation?

College "colors." How are they selected? By whom? When were they adopted? And what about nicknames for these institutions and their teams? One source of information and story material would be a manufacturer of college pennants, pins, mugs, etc. College mementoes are big business.

JUNE 17

Memorial Day in Guam . . . Bunker Hill Day (1775) . . . Birth of Igor Stravinsky (1882) . . . Amelia Earhart begins first solo flight by woman across Atlantic (1928).

Number of mail boxes in your city. Unusual anecdotes about postmen and drivers. Total miles walked by the postmen each day; mileage of post-office trucks in a month. Non-postal objects dropped into boxes by children; maintenance of boxes; new styles in mail boxes.

Microfilming of church records. The growing popularity of this method to preserve records, particularly associational minutes, and the consequent savings in storage space. The oldest records microfilmed, and also the amount of historical material which has been put on film in your community, city or state. Extend to all non-business use of microfilm records in a typical community.

Stage coach roads. The most colorful stage drivers who lived in your section. Any stage hold-ups? How the introduction of rail transportation spelled the doom of the stage coach.

JUNE 18

Declaration of war against Great Britain (1812) . . . Nation's first fly casting tournament held in Utica, New York (1861).

Families who live in more than one county. Portrait of the family that lives in a house built across county lines. How the families vote (a man's residence is where he sleeps, it has been ruled); the matter of taxes; problems about school districts. Discuss dramatic examples—half the house in "wet" and half in "dry" territory.

Antique shops. What do the experts think will be the next big "fad" in antiques—Victorian shades, milk glass, early American signs, posters and advertisements? How an antique shop collects such items; valuable articles and their history; care of antiques; effect of fads on prices.

Custom shoes. Special orders handled by stores; frequency of such orders; prices. New styles—"space" shoes, "ripple" soles; ups and downs in heels and soles; foot-care rules; step-by-step process of making shoes. Why are women's shoes so expensive—is it style or difficulties in manufacture?

JUNE 19

Samuel Colt proposes an underwater torpedo operated by electricity (1841) . . . Birth of Lou Gehrig (1903).

Courthouse clocks. How many such clocks in your county and nearby counties are in working order? The oldest of the timepieces and their original cost; rejuvenating the clocks.

Caterers and catering. How the caterer (with his staff) regularly serves hundreds (and often thousands) at various affairs; the hours required for the preparation of mammoth meals; his facilities and organization; the number of helpers, full- and part-time; his favorite recipes. Slant: A party-giver's tips for your parties.

Pneumatic tubes in business and industry. The speed with which they carry messages; dispatch of the customers' money in tubes. The earliest subways were pneumatic tubes. The tubes are used abroad—for carrying mail, vehicles, etc.

JUNE 20

West Virginia Day . . . Savannah, *first steamboat built in America to cross Atlantic, reaches Liverpool (1819).*

Hair that caught the criminal. The examination of hair in a crime laboratory in your state; the equipment used by the lab's technicians in examining stains and various materials. Slant: Hair, like fingerprints, can bring the law-breaker to justice.

An interview with a referee in bankruptcy cases. Has the number of bankruptcies increased or declined within the past twelve months? The process of declaring bankruptcy; duties of the referee; how creditors may present their claims at a hearing; settlements.

The newspaper and magazine rack at libraries. The number of newspapers and periodicals on the subscription list; the extent of their popularity; types of magazines that attract the most readers. How to find a magazine article in a library; people who "patronize" this part of library—students, browsers, researchers, those just seeking shelter.

JUNE 21

Death of John Smith (1631) . . . McCormick's reaper, the first one that is practical, is patented (1834) . . . Birth of Daniel Carter Beard (1850).

Chewing gum as a problem in theaters. Cleaning "parked" wads from seats; other headaches of theater workers, including messy candy, lost articles, etc. Slant: All the problems in a movie theater are not on the screen.

Aid to blind persons in your city. How local organizations and fraternal groups help sightless persons by organizing and sponsoring such small factory enterprises as chair-caning establishments; other ways that blind citizens have of earning income.

Junior golfers. The extent to which golfing has become a leading high school and junior high school sport; school teams and competitions; young stars who are sons or daughters of professionals—how many of the children are coached by parents? How many caddy in order to get free practice periods? Impressive scores; youngest golfers.

JUNE 22

Organic Act Day in the Virgin Islands . . . First machine for manufacturing pins is patented (J. I. Howe, 1832) . . . Germany invades Russia (1940).

Highest railroad trestle in your state. The date of its construction, and the cost; height, length, special construction problems. Have floods ever threatened it? Accidents or near-accidents on the span—is it dangerous or safer than ordinary roadbed? Other high trestles in the nation.

The old-fashioned drummer. He was a center of attention around a store in the "Gay Nineties." Discuss the splendor of his attire; his reputation as a teller of spicy jokes; the traveling salesman of today in contrast.

Information desk at a local hospital. Slant: the desk as a vital link between the patients and the public. The busiest days of the week; keeping track of patients and their condition; unusual inquiries.

JUNE 23

Government Printing Office established (1860) . . . First practical typewriter patented (C. L. Sholes, 1868).

The story behind the statue. Unique captions to go with photographs of familiar monuments. For example—how famous soldiers died, who decided to erect the memorial, who the sculptor was, where the statue was created and what its cost was. Has history bypassed men who once were memorialized with monuments?

"Okay—wash the dishes!" Interview restaurant owners to learn how often a customer does turn up with the story that he has forgotten his wallet. Do people really wash dishes in return for meals? What are the typical credit problems? What strange excuses are offered?

A day with the circulation manager of a newspaper. His task of supervising the delivery of the papers—*on time!* His outstanding problems and how he solves them. What about news delivery boys—and the manager's part in developing young carriers into good businessmen.

JUNE 24

Midsummer Day . . . San Juan Day in Puerto Rico . . . John Cabot lands at Labrador (1497) . . . Birth of Henry Ward Beecher (1813) . . . Radar detection of airplanes accomplished (1930).

Pedestrian without peer. The postman in your city or state who has the longest route. The average "life" of a pair of his shoes; whether he gets blisters from time to time; the time required to serve his patrons each day; days when the loads of mail are heaviest, and why; braving rain and cold.

An interview with the president of a beekeepers' association. The number of beekeepers in the state, and the most outstanding ones; the amount of honey produced by their bees last year; commercial markets for honey; facts and fancies about bees. What percentage of the members of the association are women?

Surnames in your city. Examine the city directory. Surnames that appear least frequently; the shortest and longest surnames; "famous" names from history, entertainment, fiction. Trends—more Smiths or fewer Smiths over the decade?

JUNE 25

John Tyler, on this day, is first President to marry while in office (1844) . . . "Custer's Last Stand" (1876).

A judo expert on a local police force. The various holds employed by the officer to subduc heavier persons; disarming attackers who have guns or knives; keeping in practice; conducting judo classes; how judo differs from *Karate.*

Tracking down automobile thieves. Actual cases in your state; the toughest ones to crack; slight clues that made possible the breaking up of "rings." Altering stolen cars in attempts to escape detection.

Photo finish! Thrilling sports contests in which the results rcmained in doubt until photographs were studied. The role of photography in sports—the pictures are not only of interest to fans but to coaches and alumni clubs.

JUNE 26

Pied Piper of Hamelin performs his feat (1284) . . . Virginia conducts lottery to raise funds; prize is 4,500 crowns (1614).

Dairy associations. Major activities of the association; promotion of milk and ice cream consumption; efforts to improve markets, conditions and income; contrasts between the old and the new dairy; predictions about the industry.

An electrical engineer looks ahead. Electrical wonders during the next quarter of a century, as envisioned by this expert; his own inventions; his most dramatic experiments; his laboratory.

Medical superstitions. (As reported by the president of a local medical society.) "Cures" for various ills; for example, the practice of stepping back across a creek for chills. "Charms" that are believed to ward off attacks—such as wearing fried onions around the neck to prevent respiratory trouble!

JUNE 27

A traffic law is enacted in New Amsterdam (1654): no speeding wagons, carts or sleighs! . . . Birth of Helen Keller (1880).

It's dynamite! Numerous uses of dynamite described, with a veteran official of a construction company as the narrator. Dynamite on construction projects: its use in blasting out foundations for buildings, removing tree stumps, wrecking old buildings. Safety procedures.

A "human fly." The tallest buildings he has scaled; his most difficult ascensions; the average fee for his climbing feats; keeping himself at top strength and agility; his favorite foods. Slant: How the stunts of a "human fly" far surpass mountain climbing in excitement and danger.

He writes under two names. An author who writes one kind of book under one name, another with a pseudonym. The volumes that have enjoyed the greatest sales; the novelist's writing habits; his plotting procedure; why he uses two names; how he chose the second.

JUNE 28

Cholera epidemic begins in New York (1832) . . . Death of James Madison (1836) . . . Birth of Richard Rodgers (1902).

Business office of a local railroad station. Slant: The behind-the-scenes work that makes the timetable possible. Business office duties, including solicitation of passenger and freight business, purchasing, printing.

A growing profession—the dental assistant. Use one girl or one class at a school, and around it build a study of this important new field—showing wages, duties, hours, qualifications for the position. What do dental patients talk about? How the assistant tries to calm the fear of children; examples of humor in a dentist's office.

What it's like to be a witness. Interview a day's (or week's) worth of witnesses at court. Were they nervous? Were their advance fears justified? Did they understand why some testimony is acceptable and some stricken from the record? Has their respect for the process of justice increased? Interview attorneys to learn why some witnesses do not want to testify—friendship, for example, or a business connection, sympathy with the suspect, dislike of police. How are witnesses paid?

JUNE 29

Birth of Peter Paul Rubens (1577) . . . Patent for revolving gun granted (1833) . . . Death of Henry Clay (1852).

Desserts around the world. From as many foreign restaurants or nationality organizations as possible, obtain recipes for favorite desserts of other countries —and whenever possible, tell the traditions and legends that surround these hot and cold sweets.

Window displays. Interview a window-display expert. Discuss "traveling displays" (many New York fashion stores rent their displays to stores in other cities on a circuit basis); rental of mannikins; costs of certain displays; how display is conceived and executed; occasional difficulties in finding props; how to make sure that displayed goods look their best.

A day with a skin-diver. The popularity of underwater swimming. Necessary equipment and training; special uses—photography, spear fishing, treasure diving, to study marine life. Clubs of skin-divers, local and national—how young are most youthful members? Safety measures; dangers; diving and "scuba" diving.

JUNE 30

Pure Food Laws enacted by Congress (1706) . . . Caster for furniture patented (1838) . . . Blondin crosses Niagara Falls on tightrope (1859).

A community frequently visited by Presidents and Vice Presidents. From George Washington to John F. Kennedy—Presidents "slept here." How the Chief Executives were entertained; their speeches; their places of lodging; why so many Chief Executives visited the area.

The highest building in your state. (Or for that matter, in *each* state. Everyone knows the Empire State Building—but how many other giant structures are quickly recognized?) Remarkable features about the skyscraper (or skyscrapers); the average number of visitors attracted weekly; the problem of washing windows; length of view from top; statistics on number of workers, companies, phones in building.

Women who serve on city councils. Their official posts; how and when they were elected to them; why they ran; their greatest achievements and their objectives. Are their husbands in politics?

JULY 1

Dominion Day in Canada . . . First adhesive postage stamps on sale (1847) . . . New York Tribune *installs linotype machine (1886) . . . First international copyright agreement becomes effective (1891).*

Blind cooks. Build a picture story around devices that help the sightless "see" in the kitchen. Braille devices on the stove; safety measures; Braille cookbooks; use of other senses—hearing, smell, touch. Other household achievements—sewing, for example—ably performed by the blind with the assistance of special devices.

Boundary quarrels. They're almost as old as the land. Choose one community, and show frequency of disputes, methods of settlement; results of surveys; markers used to denote present boundaries; shifting fences; family feuds.

"Early to bed and early to rise." How many executives and officials subscribe to this old saying? Check with as many leaders as you can to learn their habits. Get their reaction to other saws and maxims, such as "A penny saved . . ."

JULY 2

First radio communication between ground and an airplane (1917) . . . Creation of U.S. Army Air Corps (1926).

Hotel nurseries. How children are entertained during the absence of their parents; baby-sitting services. Slant: The program of hotel and motel owners to provide greater convenience for travelers, including those with children.

Blots on billboards. Interview the operator of a billboard company. What's the typical damage to signs —by weather, vandalism, accident? How often are posters changed? What are the maintenance problems? What training is needed to hang a poster? What are costs?

Religious motion pictures in churches. The equipment; sources of the films; the most popular subjects. How frequently are such programs presented? What free films are available to religious groups?

JULY 3

Bank for Savings opens in New York (1819) . . . First solo circumnavigation of world by ship completed successfully by Joshua Slocum (1898).

Youthful travelers—the children of missionaries. Their experiences abroad with their parents; customs in the countries where they make their homes; their schooling and recreation abroad; foreign toys and foods; letters to friends at home; surprises on their visits home.

For sale: old brick. How construction and demolition companies buy and sell bricks of buildings that have been torn down. And what happens to old plumbing, doors, mantles, fixtures? Demolition has become an art *and* a big business.

Do movie-goers cry? The observations of veteran theater managers. Why do people weep in a theatre but not when watching TV at home? Are emotions contagious? Do movie fans of today show more or less emotion than did those of yesteryear?

JULY 4

Declaration of Independence adopted (1776) . . . U.S. Military Academy opens (1802) . . . Birth of Nathaniel Hawthorne (1804) and Stephen Foster (1826) . . . Death of Thomas Jefferson and John Adams (1826) . . . Slavery in New York state abolished (1827) . . . First passenger railroad begun (B & O, 1828) . . . Death of James Monroe (1831) . . . Philippine Republic comes into existence (1846) . . . Birth of Calvin Coolidge (1872) and George M. Cohan (1878).

The old custom of "quilting parties." How it still is a social function in many rural communities; the output of quilts during such an occasion. Unusually old quilts owned by local citizens; the makers of the quilts; stories connected with the quilts; the attention they attract; various designs; prices.

A ghost town that has come to life again. Its original glory; causes of its decline. What's responsible for its resurrection? New industry? How attracted? What are the school and church facilities at present?

The custom of hayriding. The extent to which the beaux and belles of a given area still indulge in this pleasant form of outing. How and where to rent the equipment, costs.

JULY 5

Birth of David Farragut (1801) and Phineas T. Barnum (1810) . . . Founding of Salvation Army (1865).

What has happened to the dunce cap? Do any school teachers still use a dunce cap to shame a lazy pupil? Or are mischievous youngsters ever ordered to write "I won't talk in class" one hundred times? What about the rewards—are "gold stars" still given? Are the deserving made "monitors"? What are modern methods of praise and punishment?

Special "weeks" observed in your state. The governor's office can supply a list with background information on the various "weeks" he proclaims—discuss the ones in which he has the most interest, those given the most publicity, queens for various occasions, how and why special days and weeks are designated.

Box car data. How our railways keep exact tab on each box car; a typical route of a box car; the background and history of those freight trains we see bearing marks and symbols of almost every railroad line in the nation. How are original owners charged back for necessary repairs? The newest features of box cars.

JULY 6

Birth of John Paul Jones (1747) . . . St. Louis and London institute first international exchange of fingerprints (1905) . . . Hartford circus fire (1944).

What a city kid would learn in the 4-H. A new look at the achievements of this rural youth group, from the point of view of a non-farm youngster; the remarkable records made by our youthful agriculturists; profile of one 4-H group.

Hot dogs and soda pop. Statistics on the consumption of franks and bottled refreshments in a given period in a given place . . . baseball park, school prom or outing, a zoo—or in *all* the refreshment areas in a community on one fine day.

The conman will get you! If, that is, you don't read this feature, containing information from a Better Business Bureau representative on new frauds that fleece the gullible—with a postscript on what to do if you *do* get stung!

JULY 7

King's College (later Columbia University) opens (1754) . . . Hawaii annexed by U.S. (1898).

One foot of land. A zoölogist and a botanist describe the incredibly vast number of living things that grow or dwell *on* and *in* and *under* just one square foot of earth.

Speed cops and car tags. Are some of the cops wizards at "getting" numbers? The officers' treatment of speeders who argue; favorite alibis; how a driver is tracked down via his license plate.

After the game. The toil of stadium workers in cleaning up; finding money and other valuables. How long does it take to repair the damage done by one day's crowd? Any interesting new gadgets in use for tidying the stadium?

JULY 8

Founding of Paris (49 B.C.) . . . Liberty Bell cracks (1835) . . . Birth of John D. Rockefeller (1839) . . . Last bare-knuckle championship fight (Sullivan-Kilrain, 1889) . . . Bryan's "Cross of Gold" speech (1896).

"Fringe benefits." Describe the many "extras" offered today by industry in your community (city, state, region) to employees. Pensions, health insurance, profit-sharing plans, discount purchasing, assistance with educational costs are among these many important "plusses."

Onions and garlic. Cooks and restaurant owners offer their "sure cures" for the lingering traces of these boons to gastronomy.

Pipeline to your home. The route that must be taken by the natural gas you use in your home.

JULY 9

Birth of Elias Howe (1819) . . . Zachary Taylor dies in office (1815) . . . Birth of Daniel Guggenheim (1856) . . . Doughnut cutter patented by John F. Blondel (1872).

Don't buy "bargain" gems! A respected jeweler explains how imperfect stones, fakes and "hot" jewels are often foisted on the unsuspecting. How the jeweler recognizes real precious stones; his tests for veracity of gems and metals; the slight cost of an appraisal.

Old laws about debts. What veteran lawyers of your city say on the subject. The old law of imprisonment for debt; alimony jails.

An old-time buggy maker or dealer. His recollections of the era when buggies were in great demand: the prices of buggies in those pre-automobile days; details about the buggy-building industry; styles; the new fashions in buggy-design that raised some companies to the top, dropped others to the cellar; the handwork that went into making a buggy. Particularly lavish examples.

JULY 10

Birth of John Calvin (1509), James Whistler (1834) and Marcel Proust (1871) . . . Wyoming grants suffrage to women (1890).

What color eyes will baby have? A biologist's explanation of genes and chromosomes, and the odds that one physical factor will "dominate" another; what characteristics are inherited and which acquired; likelihood of twins or triplets.

Type faces. A feature employing many different fonts of type to show the reader how different styles convey different moods. The stories behind these types—the men who designed Goudy, Bodoni, Caslon, and so on. How type is set.

Report card time. Innovations in the reports sent home to parents. Schools that use numerals; others that use letters ranging from "A" to "F"; those that use no symbols at all, only comments; the two-grade system.

JULY 11

Birth of John Quincy Adams (1767) . . . U.S. Marine Corps created (1798) . . . Burr-Hamilton duel (1804).

Scholarships for students. In your community, city, state or region, many scholarships are offered by schools, associations, the state, industry, alumni groups, philanthropies—and some scholarships go unused for lack of applicants. A survey of opportunities.

Your city, half a century from now. Visions of the future by the mayor and members of the city council: predictions of changes in industry and transportation; what the officials foresee in terms of population increase and the city's area; changes the mayor and councilmen would like to witness most of all.

Lawn hints and helps. Advice from an expert on weeding, watering, fertilizers, dry patches, lawn supplements; a survey of new products for the lawn; free advice and assistance available to the home-owner.

JULY 12

Birth of Julius Caesar (100 B.C.) and Henry David Thoreau (1817) . . . Patent granted for paper bag manufacturing machine (1859).

Greeting card collections. Lovely old Christmas, Valentine's Day, and other holiday cards owned by a collector.

A harbormaster's duties. His responsibilities for the safe movement of vessels and cargoes; the devices he uses to keep the traffic moving safely; such special problems as storms, dangerous cargoes, speed-happy powerboat enthusiasts.

Flying windmills. New uses for helicopters—on the farm; in emergency work, short-haul postal work, traffic control; as "cavalry of the sky" for defense. A pilot's report on his varied activities in a whirlybird.

JULY 13

Nathan Bedford Forrest's Birthday in Tennessee . . . Northwest Ordinance passed (1787) . . . New York City adopts legislation regulating pawnbrokers (1812).

Women's footwear down the years. Visit a museum and inspect ancient shoes. Footwear a century ago; the period of high shoes, which declined as women entered the business world.

Today's heroes. Interview a high school graduating class to discover their idols in contemporary life. Do the boys and girls agree on their selections? What do the teachers think about these selections?

How "X" highway has changed! Choose one major route, and describe all the changes in its complexion in recent years, for better or for worse—new roadside establishments, billboards, speed laws, safety measures, populated places along the way; how nearby communities have gained or suffered; daily traffic compared, now and then.

JULY 14

Bastille Day in France . . . Tape measure patented by A. J. Fellows (1868).

Vital work of a hospital histologist. An interview that provides insight into the dramatic work of the medical expert responsible for microscopic examination of tissues, and that shows pathology's role in modern medicine.

Pro and con on hitchhiking. Students explain why they're for it; law enforcement authorities discuss the many dangers; an auto insurance expert explains how hitchhiking jeopardizes the driver.

The business of moving houses. Interview the operator of a housemoving company in your section. Details about the work and methods, the time required for removals, the largest structures that have been moved, those moved the greatest distances, and the most difficult removals.

JULY 15

St. Swithin's Day . . . Birth of Rembrandt (1606) . . . First Buddhist temple in U.S. established in Los Angeles (1904).

Original ways to apply for a job. Ask personnel directors of large stores, newspapers, advertising agencies and factories in your area to describe the most unusual stunts used by position-seekers; odd methods that clicked.

Highway signs. The designs of these signs and what they signify. How recognition of signs is included in examinations for applicants of driving licenses; damage to signs; efforts to standardize American signs, as in Europe; how most legible colors for signs are selected after long testing.

A day with a bookmobile driver. Number of miles she travels monthly, and the quantity and types of books circulated during the period; the most popular authors at present; the subject's own preferences in literature. Has television affected the popularity of the "library on wheels?"

JULY 16

Birth of Joshua Reynolds (1723) and Mary Baker Eddy (1821) . . . First atom bomb test, Alamagordo (1945).

Pioneer churches that meted out hard justice to flaunters of religious laws. The question of Sunday traveling; religious uproars; expulsion of members from churches; ministers who fell into displeasure with their congregations.

Food for the public. How does a restaurant owner know what to buy—and in what quantities? How does he establish prices? His state restaurant association provides much of this vital data. Interview an executive of such a group to see how this expert helps remove some of the gambles and grumbles in his field.

Bird shelters. Many of the feeders and houses for our feathered friends are little palaces. Do a photo spread on unusual shelters, emphasizing how protection is provided against looters and predators.

JULY 17

Muñoz Rivera's Birthday in Puerto Rico . . . Florida formally ceded by Spain to U.S. (1821) . . . The first photograph of a star (Vega) made at Harvard (1850).

Ice—a big business. From ice cubes for a party to ice for industry, there are many uses for the stuff we skid and slip on (for free) during the cold winter months. How ice is manufactured and distributed; automatic ice-vending machines. Sidelight: Are many iceboxes still in use?

Strange souvenirs. Photographs and description of items brought back by travelers returning from abroad and from other parts of the United States—with particular emphasis on what youngsters hauled back with them.

A toy-lending library. The librarian and her assistants. How this "library" is operated on the same plan as a book-lending library; the number and types of toys available; the most popular among children; the membership of the library.

JULY 18

Nero fiddles while Rome burns (64) . . . First advertisement to occupy a half-page appears in New York's Weekly Journal *(1743) . . . "Wrong Way" Corrigan's flight (1938).*

Raising milk goats. Enterprising farmers who engage in goat raising on a scientific basis—not for the meat but for the milk, which is used extensively to feed hospital patients. The importance of goat milk as an aid to infants and invalids.

An interview with a spider expert. The number of spiders in his collection, and his studies of their habits; characteristics of this insect; the question of spider bites; "writing" spiders.

Dedications by authors. A day of research in the library will yield fascinating dedications—some loving, some bitingly sharp, some funny.

JULY 19

Birth of Samuel Colt (1814) and Edmund Degas (1834) . . . First convention of women advocating woman suffrage meets at Seneca Falls (1848), and Amelia Jenks Bloomer wears "bloomers" in public for first time.

Instinct at work. A round-up of fascinating actions performed by animals operating purely on instinct. Examples—the salmon swimming upstream, the bird teaching a fledgling to fly, the dog eating grass to settle an aching tummy. Get other examples from veterinarians, pet shop managers, pet owners.

An exchange student in your community. His impressions of this country; his life at home; the courses he is taking and why; his observations on fellow-students; his opinion on whether we're doing a good job of promulgating democratic concepts.

Knots and splices. Let the reader learn the ropes as he reads this interview with a sailor (or a Boy Scout leader) who explains the half-hitch and granny. Knots that make home packaging easier; ties for the fisherman; splices of practical value.

JULY 20

Confederate Congress holds first session (Richmond, 1861) . . . Cigarette tax-stamps ordered on packages (1868).

Utilities "trouble shooter." The man who repairs felled or broken lines after storms: dangerous assignments; worst storms, line-wise, that he recalls; automobile accidents that result in toppled power poles, thereby creating dangerous situations; what to do if you pass such an accident—or if you're involved in one.

Reading a label. A home economics expert tells what we should look for before we buy—an explanation of all the data on labels on fabrics, packaged foods, household products.

The dredging of historic rivers. Have such operations in your state brought to light interesting relics—cannon balls, for example, or vessels previously lost without trace? But of even greater interest is the full-time work that must go on to keep the river navigable today. Describe a day on a dredger.

JULY 21

Liberation Day in Guam . . . Battle of Bull Run Creek (1861) . . . Birth of Ernest Hemingway (1898) . . . John Boettner makes emergency jump to safety by parachute from a balloon (1919).

Let's follow a bill through Congress. The human, the mechanical, the traditional aspects of enacting legislation. Follow a bill sponsored by a local representative or Senator, watching it go from the "hopper" through committee to debate and final votes in both houses.

"Take a letter, Miss Jones." Estimates are that it costs from $2.00 to $5.00 when an executive in a large company dictates a letter. Expense factors include: salaries of executive and secretary, equipment used, stationery, postage, share of overhead, filing time and space, and so on. Survey costs in your community. What's being done to reduce expenses?

Dog shows as a business. Prize winners and how they are readied for the shows; veteran judges; entrants from the longest distances; prizes; the most popular breeds in the shows.

JULY 22

Wiley Post completes first around-the-world solo flight (1933) . . . John Dillinger shot (1934).

Oddest items ever pawned, as recalled by a veteran pawnbroker. Did the pawnshop customers return to redeem the articles? How pawnbrokers help the police by keeping record books that contain descriptions of what may be stolen items.

The popularity of rummage sales. The magnetic appeal of the sale of a person's household effects to neighbors and friends. How church organizations and clubs sponsor such sales for the raising of funds. Are some possessions sold by mistake?

You're responsible! An expert in liability insurance explains the myriad ways in which landlord and tenant can be legally and financially responsible for accidents and injuries that range from a housemaid's tumble off a stepstool to nips by the pet dog; what kind of protection is available; costs. Case histories.

JULY 23

First swimming school opens in Boston (1827) . . . Death of Ulysses S. Grant (1885) . . . Railroad car with an observation dome in service (1945).

The light that never fails. Men who work in a lighthouse; their search and rescue operations; famous lighthouses; innovations, including new bulbs, radar, radio contact; how lighthouse keepers fight gloom and loneliness.

Reading lips. How the deaf are taught to "hear" by sight; methods of instruction. Do the deaf ever yield to the temptation to "eavesdrop"? Interview an instructor to gain insight into his methods of training, average time required to learn lip-reading.

The cost of living. Translate monthly government statistics into the actual expenditures made today and yesterday by a specific family. Does their present higher income go as far as more modest wages did some years ago? What are their budgetbreakers?

JULY 24

Pioneer Day in Utah . . . Birth of Simón Bolivar (1783) . . . R. M. Hoe patents rotary printing press (1847) . . . Birth of Amelia Earhart (1898).

Life on a houseboat. Interview a family who spend their vacations—or live all year—on the river: their facilities for comfort and cooking; repairs afloat; how it feels not to worry about mowing and crabgrass.

Revealing ink blots. A psychiatrist describes the Rorschach Test, how it was discovered almost by accident, and how it is used in psychodiagnostic work.

Tax returns can be funny. Humorous examples cited by the city and county tax-takers; odd reports turned in by taxpayers; oft repeated jokes about taxes.

JULY 25

Constitution Day in Puerto Rico . . . First railroad accident in U.S. (on Granite Railway, Massachusetts, 1832) . . . Paper collar patented by Walter Hunt (1854).

Vacation on a dude ranch. The folks who spend their holidays on horseback; entertainment at the ranch; rodeo fun; chuckwagon dining; learning to ride and rope. Locations and costs of dude ranch vacationing.

Kid songs and doggerel. A round-up of the songs and poems recited by youngsters as they skip rope, bounce a ball, play pick-up jacks and other games in which words are as important as actions.

Remember rationing? A look back at the ration books, stamps and cards of World War II. Pictures of the stickers affixed to our cars, indicating our priorities for gas and tires.

JULY 26

Benjamin Franklin appointed first Postmaster (1775) . . . Birth of George Bernard Shaw (1856) . . . Death of Sam Houston (1863).

An editor's advice to amateur publicists. Ask a newspaper editor to tell the reader how to get news about organizational events, elections, or special drives into his paper. Do's and don'ts for the volunteer publicist.

How to photograph flowers. Advice by a local photographer who is an expert in taking pictures of flowers. Flowers most difficult to photograph; the most beautiful flowers.

"See a specialist." A hospital administrator lists and defines the many medical specialties available to patients today.

JULY 27

Barbosa's Birthday in Puerto Rico . . . U.S. Department of Foreign Affairs created (1789) . . . Orville Wright's flight at Fort Myer (1909).

How to recognize poison ivy. And poison oak—along with those other plants, shrubs and flowers that can make one regret a stroll in the fields and woods. New drugs used to cure or diminish pain and discomfort caused by poisonous plants.

Political parties. Most people can think of just two or three—but over *thirty* parties presented candidates for the presidency in 1960. And many of them were odd indeed! Discuss party names and platforms, number of votes they achieved, present status. Your news peg is the fact that this week is "convention time" in presidential-election years.

Dog accessories. Big-city dog-supply shops now sell—both across the counter and by mail—such items as: mink coats for poodles, jeweled collars and leashes with real gems, doggie booties, whistles the dog can hear but people cannot, luxurious beds for our four-footed friends, and so on. An amusing approach might be a country dog-city dog dialogue.

JULY 28

Founder of playgrounds (Joseph Lee) honored . . . Vermont constitution—providing for universal manhood suffrage—adopted by Vermont (1777).

What makes a caddy unhappy? The ten greatest irritations for caddies. Keeping silent despite the faults of the golfers. Are women devotees of the links more considerate of caddies than men? Caddies who long to become golf professionals.

"Confucius say." Most of us know little about what the ancient Chinese philosophers really did say and teach. Interview an Orientalist or philosophy professor to gain insight into the teachings of Confucius, Lao Tse, and others.

Table-top photography. An exponent of the tricks and startling effects of this form of camera magic describes and demonstrates his art.

JULY 29

Birth of Booth Tarkington (1864) . . . Police training school of F.B.I. initiated (1935).

Plant propagation. A horticulturist provides helpful information on grafting and on "bits that grow big." Photographs illustrate the best ways to increase plants.

Our changing playgrounds. Discuss the new, radically-different free-form structures, tunnels, mazes, piles, and "jungle gyms" that can be found in modern playgrounds, replacing old-fashioned sandboxes and seesaws. Interview a member of the National Recreation Association for a description of new approaches to community play centers.

An interview with the business manager of a penitentiary. Slant: The prison must be operated on a businesslike basis in addition to serving as a place of punishment and rehabilitation. Daily and monthly cost of operation: major items of expense; revenue from the manufacture of products; the prison factory.

JULY 30

Birth of Emily Brontë (1818) . . . New York Yacht Club organized (1844) . . . Birth of Henry Ford (1863) . . . Death in action of Joyce Kilmer (1918).

A medical "detail man." He works for a pharmaceutical or medical supply house, and his job is to keep physicians up-to-date on new drugs and health devices. Interview one of these specialists in sales and science.

Fugitives who met their Waterloo at railroad or bus stations. Famous criminals captured at terminals; alert ticket sellers; how the police set traps. Do most fugitives surrender without resistance when cornered?

The caboose of a freight train. The equipment; preparation of meals; typical menus for the railroad men. A veteran cook and his common and uncommon experiences.

JULY 31

First patent issued by U.S. granted to Samuel Hopkins for process of making potash; it was signed by Washington, Jefferson and Edmund Randolph (1790) . . . Opening of Idlewild Airport (1948) . . . Death of Robert Taft (1953).

"Only child." How do some "only children" who are now mature feel about having been the one kid in the family? Do youngsters from large families ever envy the only child?

Optical illusions. A round-up of tricks of the eye. An expert explains why seeing is not believing in these instances.

Hints for picnickers. What to take in the basket and as equipment. Games for the family on a picnic. What city folks on a picnic in the country must avoid (berries, mushrooms, angry bulls, trespassing).

AUGUST 1

Colorado Day . . . Birth of William Clark (1770) . . . Whiskey Rebellion begins in Pennsylvania (1794) . . . Birth of Herman Melville (1819) . . . San Francisco cable car goes into operation (1873).

Origami and other paper work. The Japanese art of paper-folding has invaded these shores. Paper-folding tricks the reader can perform. Paper sculpture, flowers and party decorations. The newspaper printer's famous "paper hat."

Pardons. Last-minute or year-end pardons by governors and Presidents.

Fainting in the courtroom. Recollections of a veteran judge: expressions on defendants' faces when verdicts and sentences are pronounced; female defendants who show no inhibition in their grief and disappointment; instances in which medical attention is required; last-minute confessions; suicide and escape attempts.

AUGUST 2

First public letter boxes installed (Boston and New York, 1858) . . . Army Ambulance Corps established (1862) . . . Death of Alexander Graham Bell (1922) and Warren Harding (1923).

Store protection services. Operations of a central office that installs alarm systems in stores and plants and speeds to the scene at any indication of intrusion. How the service spots its men, radio-cars, and sub-offices so that no customer is more than minutes away.

My trip to Alaska. An "as-told-to-you" report by a traveler just back from the 49th state—or any other area of the world in which Americans are deeply interested today: Africa, Israel, the Far East.

Early symptoms of alcoholism. A medical expert—or a member of A.A.—discusses some of the signals that can warn: "Danger—alcoholism ahead!" For example—drinking in the morning, "blacking out" frequently, "stealing" extra shots while acting as host.

AUGUST 3

Christopher Columbus sets sail from Spain (1492) . . . Birth of Hamilton Fish (1808) . . . American Canoe Association formed (1880) . . . Death of Thorstein Veblen (1929).

Church mergers. There is a trend toward consolidation among denominations. How do these mergers work out at the neighborhood level, in local churches? Interview ministers of merging denominations to learn the many significant aspects of these groupings.

Routing dangerous trucks. Disasters in the past have made highway officials alert to the risks involved when trucks bearing explosives or inflammables must cross bridges, go through tunnels, or pass through crowded areas. Discuss local, city, state regulations that prevent catastrophes.

Chauffeurs. Who rates a chauffeur in your city or state government? What other jobs are filled by the driver? Percentage of drivers in your area who hold special licenses for chauffeuring. Are tests for these drivers more stringent than those given ordinary drivers?

AUGUST 4

John Peter Zenger acquitted of libel charges (1735) . . . Chautauqua Organization formed (1874).

Music and dance festivals. A look at the special programs that will be presented in your region in coming months. The artists, sponsors, works to be performed. Dates and admission data.

Ballet terminology and annotation. While covering the above story, you can begin to gather information on the fascinating new system of "writing down" the intricate movements of a ballet corps. And to do this, you'll have to explain, in general, the meaning of the various ballet "positions" and the special terminology of dance.

Is it a bargain? A Better Business Bureau representative explains some of the phrases that can make bad buys sound like bargains. For example, all these phrases make it *seem* as if an item has actually been marked down in price: "Comparable value . . ."—"Would ordinarily be . . ."—"Ordinarily sells for as much as . . ."

AUGUST 5

Birth of Guy de Maupassant (1850) . . .
First cable under Atlantic (1858).

Foreign language newspapers in the United States. Hundreds of them are published in the nation. The most popular features of these newspapers; how they are changing as new generations come along, unable to speak or read the language of the old country.

Making eyeglasses. The grinding of each lens; polishing; special lenses for particular needs; steps in making bifocals. The training necessary for this exacting work. Imported lenses.

Battle of the beetles. There are wars going on across the country in which beetles are the fighters. An extension service agent discusses the damage done by *khapra beetles*; the way in which helpful *tiger beetles* are used to benefit the farmer. The part played by beetles in goatweed control.

AUGUST 6

Gertrude Ederle swims Channel (1926) . . . Judge Crater disappears (1930) . . . First atomic bomb dropped (Hiroshima, 1945).

Paint-it-yourself tips. A decorator, paint store proprietor, or paint company representative offers helpful hints: the right brush or roller for the job; the various paint bases, and which to select for what purpose; preventing the paints from separating in the can; brush care; storing paint-soaked rags in cans.

How to win an argument. Pointers in persuasion as supplied by a lawyer, arbitrator, star salesman, advertising copywriter and politician.

Armored car—from the inside! How many men inside the impressive truck that carries money to and from the banks? With what kind of "shootin' irons" —sub-machine guns? Pistols? Rifles? How thick is the "armor" on the vehicle? Are the trucks radio-equipped? How good is the vision from those tiny slits in back and sides?

AUGUST 7

Birth of Nathanael Greene (1742) . . . Church services for deaf inaugurated in New York City (1859) . . . Revolving door patented (1888).

Smörgasbord! A Swedish cook tells us how to duplicate the wonders of this feast—describing the various fish dishes, patés, salads, cold cuts, cheeses, vegetables and meats to present, and offering recipes for such typical delights as Swedish meatballs and hot beans.

Pre-fabs. In pictures and captions, show the incredible speed with which the new pre-fabricated summer homes are assembled and made ready for immediate occupancy. Costs, special features, optional equipment.

Home bulletin-boards. A survey of the notes, invitations, old bills, clippings, reminders, and oddments found on the bulletin boards in several homes.

AUGUST 8

Spanish Armada destroyed (1588) . . . D. B. Wesson patents metal cartridge (1854) . . . Thomas Alva Edison patents mimeograph (1876).

Business gifts. Now's the time that businessmen get started on their Christmas shopping—for calendars imprinted with the company name, for other desk accessories, for novelties that range from electric pencil sharpeners to miniatures of the company product. Do a profile of a leading purveyor of business gifts.

Butterflies by the thousand. There's more to this hobby than collection, preservation and mounting. Many people use butterfly wings to "paint" pictures, or as decorations for plates and lamp bases and vases. Photos of some of the objects so decorated, along with a description of the ways in which the artist acquires his unique supplies.

Be an expert meat carver! What's the good of cooking that steak to a turn on the barbecue—if you don't slice it right? A chef explains (and photographs of him illustrate) how to carve beef, lamb, veal and fowl.

AUGUST 9

Birth of Izaac Walton (1593) . . . Jesse Owens wins four prizes at Berlin Olympics (1936) . . . Second atomic bomb dropped (Nagasaki, 1945).

Foam rubber. The "do-it-yourself" addict is enchanted by the thought of using foam rubber when he re-upholsters chairs or makes a modern bench or bed. But foam rubber comes in many sizes, thicknesses and grades of resiliency, and many special facts must be known. And so *you* get an expert to explain and demonstrate.

Salt and pepper. We take them for granted. Where do they come from? Why the return to ground pepper or peppercorns crushed in a mortar? Relate some of the romance of pepper and piracy, salt rebellions, old-time methods of providing salt for the tables of the world.

How a lawyer keeps up with decisions. The publications, briefs, reports and digests available to attorneys so that they're always up-to-date on significant cases and decisions. Similar services for the physician and other professions.

AUGUST 10

Birth of Jay Cooke (1821) . . . Chicago incorporated as a village (1833) . . . Boston appoints first milk inspectors in nation (1859) . . . Birth of Herbert Hoover (1874).

Let's have a clam bake! Have an expert tell the reader all he needs to know about preparing the pit, selecting the foods, steaming, serving—all, in fact, but whom to invite.

Professional guide. He might be a fisherman's guide or one who shepherds tourists about—a hunter or an expert at the state capital or a museum. Or you might want to do a round-up feature on the surprisingly large number of professional guides at work in your community, city or state.

Horns and antlers. With photographs showing only sharp horns, blunt ones—indeed, all you can locate in a day at zoo or library—challenge the reader to distinguish the animal by his head gear.

AUGUST 11

Patent granted to Harvey Hubbell for electric light socket with pull chain (1896) . . . First radio SOS (Araphoe, *off Cape Hatteras, 1909) . . . Death of Andrew Carnegie (1919).*

"Local hits." Many books, records and entertainers have achieved local fame, but are not nationally known. Are there singers or musicians in your section whose records are community-wide bestsellers, but are little-known elsewhere? What books are state-wide leaders in stores and libraries? Cite stories of local successes that went on to national fame.

The story of a newspaper. From leg-man on a story to delivery of the paper. Follow one story all the way through, minute by minute; show that the popular concept of a "deadline" is wrong—there are many new deadlines every few minutes, on the editorial desk and in the mail-room, where the presses roll and in the company garage.

Raining cats and dogs? It's not as unlikely as it sounds! A university meteorologist or the local weatherman can describe hail storms in the summer, and times when far stranger things fell from the sky in freak storms.

AUGUST 12

Isaac Singer patents sewing machine (1851) . . . Hawaii formally annexed (1895) . . . Air mail service, New York City to Washington, established on regular basis (1918).

Lifeboat luxuries. Modern lifeboats are better equipped than the vessels in which 16th century explorers journeyed to these shores. Show and explain the safety devices, signals, rations and other equipment placed in emergency boats carried today by passenger and military ships.

Photo retouching. The art of eliminating nature's oversights; wrinkles, moles, freckles disappear when the retoucher goes to work! His services in portrait photography, and his work for business, industry and the press. Is photo coloring a dying art?

Reflexes. Why the physician raps your knee or tickles the sole of a baby's foot. How reflexes show the state of your health. A physician explains the many reflex tests that help him in diagnoses.

AUGUST 13

Manteo, first Indian convert to Protestantism, baptized into faith (1587).

New frontiers in mental research. An interview with the superintendent of a state hospital. New methods of treatment yielding better results; testing techniques. Into what new areas in government and business will psychological testing go?

Life of a Washington correspondent. A typical day for a Washington correspondent of a given newspaper; the sources of his news; scoops he has scored. The number of women correspondents in Washington. Gossip, rumor, social life.

The ROTC. How college undergraduates receive military training on the campus. Special Armed Forces Day parades and competitions. An outstanding ROTC band. Training in use of rifles.

AUGUST 14

Victory Day in Rhode Island . . . World War II Memorial Day in Arkansas . . . Patent granted for electric motor (1888) . . . Social Security Act passed (1935) . . . End of World War II (1945).

Ship models in a bottle. A hobbyist allows you to photograph and describe in detail his painstaking efforts to make an accurate model; the ingenious manner in which it is slipped through the neck of the bottle and then set up in final proud display.

Soap sculpture. Things for the kids to make and do with bars of soap and soap lather, as described (and demonstrated) by an arts and crafts teacher.

Monkeys as pets. A pet-shop owner will help you find a family that boasts a monkey as a pet. All about the furry little fellow—his diet, monkey business, where he sleeps, pranks and exercise, clever tricks.

AUGUST 15

Birth of Sir Walter Raleigh (1771) . . . Will Rogers, Wiley Post killed in plane crash (1935) . . . India and Pakistan come into existence (1947).

What our ancestors wore. The summer and winter attire of the pioneer inhabitants of your state. Clothes in a museum; quotes on clothing from old letters and diaries. Spinning wheels preserved in your area.

A leading supplier of Christmas trees. He's getting ready now! How a forest owner prepares for the distribution and sales of trees for the Yuletide season. The most popular sizes and probable prices. Does the subject ship a large number of trees to other counties or states?

Telephone "hogging." Telephone "hogs" on party lines are just as common as road "hogs." The telephone company's plans for substituting private wires. Subscribers registering complaints to the office; terminating the telephone service of abusers. Kinds of complaints—i.e., children who consume too much time and adults who use profane language.

AUGUST 16

Battle of Bennington (1777) . . . Gold discovered in Alaska (1896) . . . Babe Ruth dies (1948).

An interview with a draft board clerk. His day-by-day activities; the voluminous files in the office. Do most young men welcome the opportunity to broaden their horizons, literally and figuratively, by entering the armed forces? Trying to locate persons. The matter of deferrals.

Sunspots—what they mean to us. Strange things may occur in radio transmission, overseas telephone conversations, wireless transmission at "sunspot time." A meteorologist explains this phenomenon.

A cement factory. The raw materials used in the manufacture of cement; the various processes of production; the history of cement.

AUGUST 17

Birth of Davy Crockett (1786) . . . First public bath with showers opens in New York (1891) . . . Fulton's steam boat makes first trip (1907).

Patio pleasures. Step-by-step directions in building a patio or terrace (or *lanai,* as the West Coasters and Hawaiians say)—showing how one family is actually doing it themselves. Followed by ways to enjoy this outdoor improvement—barbeques, terrace parties, family fun in the sun.

Mass madness. Times in your community's past when emotions ran wild, and most residents shared elation, fear, panic, bewilderment—as so many Americans did with the Orson Welles "invasion from Mars," or as the result of false armistice reports, or rumors of the escape of wild animals from a zoo or circus.

Ship silhouettes. A review of ship recognition through masts and rigging, sails. The various "classes" of sailboat. Interview with an old salt who describes the sailor's chores aloft.

AUGUST 18

Birth of Virginia Dare (1587) . . . Women suffrage amendment approved by Congress (1920).

"Fatigue" in metals. An engineer explains how, in the construction of anything from airplanes to bridges to skyscrapers, one must understand "fatigue," stress and fracture of metals. The intricate scientific, mathematical methods to arrive at the needed information.

Automobile driver tests. The most extraordinary experiences at the highway department quarters; the worst faults of young people seeking a driving license; the oldest applicants; parts of the tests that are the toughest.

Marinas—hotels in the harbor. Close-up (or a trip's worth) of one of the motel-restaurant-and-gas-station combinations at the water's edge. They supply food, shelter, service and a place for companionship for boating enthusiasts. And marinas now provide a network of "rest stops" for voyagers along coasts and many inland waterways.

AUGUST 19

National Aviation Day (birth of Orville Wright, 1871) . . . Daughters of American Revolution organized (1890) . . . F. W. Koons is first American soldier in World War II to land on French soil (1942).

Calypso singers—reporters in song. How these Caribbean minstrels weave news events and personality comments into their extemporaneous ditties. Show how a calypso singer (or student of this song style) might build local (city, state, regional) events into a barbed ballad.

The compass. We all know what they are—but how many of us know how to use one? Instructions in various uses of various kinds of compasses from a Boy Scout, sports car driver, pilot, military man and sailor.

Swamp life. Ingenious residents of marsh and moor have come up with unique vehicles, home designs, techniques for fishing and hunting that simplify their daily life. A report by a visitor or former dweller in bog lands.

AUGUST 20

Alaska discovered (by Bering, 1741) . . . Birth of Benjamin Harrison (1833) . . . First successful automatic dial system for telephones patented (1896).

"My trip to Russia." An interview with a traveler who has just returned from the Soviet. Questions asked Americans by the Russians. Sights that impressed him. Ease or difficulties in travel.

Safe deposit boxes. Why they *are* super-safe. What happens when you lose your keys (it's the only time lock-cracking is legal in a bank!). Tax deductions for charges; keeping a list of the contents of the box.

An interview with a cattle auctioneer. How a cattle auction packs more fun than the antics and sideshows of a county fair. Scenes on the floor; the chant of the auctioneer, who's never at a loss for words or sounds. Bidding signs given by the crowd. Cattle prices at present.

AUGUST 21

Lincoln-Douglas debates begin (1858) . . .
American Bar Association organized (1878).

Archery hunting. This "new" sport is one of the oldest under the sun! The scenes of the hunts; the biggest "kills"; specialized archery groups interested primarily in the crossbow; distance the arrow can travel; velocity; modern arrowheads.

Death certificates. The need for such a certificate when a person dies, as explained by the president of the local medical society. Determining the exact cause of death.

Salad days. A dietician or nutritionist urges more salads on the American dinner table, and provides favorite recipes. Famous salads of famous restaurants. Exotic salads from Hawaii, Italy and France.

AUGUST 22

Birth of Claude Debussy (1862) . . . Soap in liquid form patented by William Sheppard (1865) . . . "Teddy" Roosevelt becomes first President to ride in an automobile on this day (1902).

"Soldiers without swords." A profile of a Salvation Army group; their important work in rehabilitation and charity. The famous Army bands.

Sand castles. A picture story of a splendid sand-structure built on a beach by a band of youngsters. Captions to be the excited words of the kids as they dig moats and tunnels, carve out roads for a rubber ball. Last picture—the tide comes in.

Sharks. Fact and fancy about these terrors of the sea. Experiences of shark fishers and skin-divers. Shark scares, justified or not.

AUGUST 23

First bank clearing house organized (1853) . . . Birth of Oliver Hazard Perry (1858) . . . New York's Fifth Avenue Hotel becomes first to install an elevator (1859).

How to increase the attendance of a Sunday School class. The most effective plans used in your city; originators of the ideas; Sundays with the highest attendance.

A mule market. Old Maud stubbornly refuses to make her exit in spite of the advent of mechanical farming. Interview a veteran mule dealer. Prices of mules through the years.

From "baa" to beautiful coat. The story of a sheep farm; care and management; bathing and shearing; protecting sheep from predators; the market for wool and lamb linings; how and where processing takes place.

AUGUST 24

British burn Capitol (1814) . . . Patent granted for waffle iron (1869).

"My reference shelf." Books turned to most often by notables or local persons in various professions. What do they keep alongside their dictionary, Bible, thesaurus?

Skunks as pets and pests. These little fellows give us fair warning before they attack: a naturalist or sportsman explains what to do and what not to do when suddenly confronted by a skunk. A pet shop manager talks about skunks as pets and explains the deskunking process.

How to use a slide rule. The mystifying slipsticks look like black magic until explained. Step-by-step instruction from a teacher of mathematics or engineering.

AUGUST 25

New Orleans founded (1718) . . . Birth of Bret Harte (1839) . . . U.S. troops liberate Paris (1944).

Name writing on wet pavement. Have people lost their zest for writing their names on wet pavement during the past decade or so? Methods found effective in curbing the practice.

A day with a social worker. Her daily schedule of counseling, interviewing, arranging for assistance and rehabilitation. Training for various types of casework—with children, the aged, the handicapped, the indigent. The educational and emotional demands of her profession.

Tall girls' club. They've banded together—mostly to swap clothes and dates! A group of 5′10″-ers-and-up on a campus. Their problems in finding attractive clothes in proper sizes; the tired old jokes they hear too frequently.

AUGUST 26

New York Sun *receives first news dispatch by cable (1858) . . . Birth of Dr. Lee De Forest (1873).*

A sports car rally. Not a race, but a test of driving skill—requiring the ability to follow complex and mystifying directions; to keep to steady speeds; to observe every traffic law. Duties of driver and "navigator"—often husband-and-wife teams.

"Faking with figures." A researcher, statistician or mathematics expert demonstrates how figures can be used to tell a tale that's not quite true—the kind we occasionally suspect when reading some political speeches and advertisements.

Use of the life net by firemen. The number of lives saved by use of the net; testing it from time to time; trying to calm persons trapped in a burning building.

AUGUST 27

Birth of Confucius (550 B.C.) . . . First steamboat to carry a man, built by John Fitch, paddled down Delaware River (1787) . . . Birth of Theodore Dreiser (1871).

Flight surgeon. Interview a medical officer attached to one of the flight services, or a member of the Aero Medical Association. Special problems of medicine in the supersonic age. Space medicine. Airborne hospitals.

What a travel agent can do for you. There's no charge for the endless services a skilled travel agent can and does perform—in making reservations, arranging tours, securing theatre tickets, suggesting exciting side-visits.

Nuts to you! The many varieties of nuts on sale in specialty shops and supermarkets. Where grown. Gourmet recipes involving nuts—"almond amandine," for example. New nuts on the market from Hawaii, South America.

AUGUST 28

Birth of Goethe (1749) and Tolstoi (1828) . . . Operations commence at U.S. Engraving and Printing Bureau (1862).

A gal's softball team. Their exploits; travel stories; the quick change from glamour girl to athlete; how the team members became interested in the sport; their opinion of abilities of men's teams playing a similar circuit.

Loading baggage on a plane. The new "capsules" into which the traveler's luggage is loaded, saving time for all concerned. Why weight limits? What should *not* be packed when one flies by air? Automation at the airport.

Your pet cat. Helpful hints from breeders, vets, exhibitors on care, training, feeding, breeding, showing: how to prevent damage to furniture; where to buy or adopt a kitten; the pedigreed cat versus the alley cat.

AUGUST 29

First Indian reservation established (New Jersey, 1798) . . . Death of Brigham Young (1877) . . . Birth of Oliver Wendell Holmes (1894).

A pastor who performs marriage counseling. Many ministers now meet the engaged couple regularly for several weeks before the ceremony. Others conduct informal "classes" for several couples. The value of these sessions; comments by the engaged pairs. The special training of the minister for this work.

When a small business needs money. How, where, when and to whom a small retailer or manufacturer goes when his business requires additional working capital. City, state and federal agencies; banks, associations.

Fabrics that won't stain or burn. New developments, explained by a fabric manufacturer, for treating textiles so that the most grievous stains can simply be wiped away, and the hazards of burning drapes and curtains reduced by fireproofing. Innovations that do not alter the appearance of the fabric.

AUGUST 30

Huey P. Long's Birthday in Louisiana . . . Cleopatra commits suicide (30 B.C.) . . . First Congregational Church in U.S. established (1637).

World's champion giver of books. A representative of the American Bible Society describes the far-reaching activities of the group in donating and distributing copies of the Bible at home and abroad.

Fun with foods. Photographs and descriptions of gay little things the kiddies can make with packaged and dried foods—for example, necklaces and bracelets of uncooked macaroni, figures made of carrots and apples, chains of dried watermelon seeds. A kindergarten teacher will have many more suggestions!

Comic strips are his business. An interview with the writer or illustrator of a daily or magazine comic strip feature. His working schedule. Searching for ideas. Letters from readers. "Boners" caught by his fans. Models. How color comics are produced.

AUGUST 31

Birth of Arthur Godfrey (1903) . . . Election returns broadcast (in Detroit) for first time (1920).

Does the movie affect the appetite? Do different types of motion pictures affect our yearning for popcorn or candy? Do we eat more during a tense suspense film than during a light comedy? The concessionaire at a drive-in discusses emotions versus intake.

Brotherhood Day. A clear look at the contributions to the community (city, state, region, country) made by minority groups that are sometimes the unfortunate object of intolerance.

"Best renters at the library." What books are borrowed most at the public library in a given community? What were the "best renters" five, ten and forty years ago?

SEPTEMBER 1

Death of William Clark (1838) . . . First Pullman sleeping car put in service (Bloomington to Chicago, 1859) . . . Second World War begins (1939).

The war against ragweed. What is being done in your city, state or region to lower the pollen count —and prevent, for many people, a month of wheezing and sneezing. And (as related by a health official) what the actual pollen counts were in representative areas last year.

Dramatic new churches. Architects and designers have recently revolutionized church design. Show a sampling of some of these new structures, and explain how ease and quiet and "expandability" are built into them. How church members felt about the plans at first—and now.

Wingless wonder. At an air base you can see, photograph and perhaps even "fly" a plane that never leaves the ground—and yet duplicates for the trainee all the sensations, hazards and conditions of actual flight. The gadget itself, how it works, its contribution to the budget and pilot safety.

SEPTEMBER 2

Great Fire of London (1666) . . . U.S. Treasury organized (1789) . . . Birth of Eugene Field (1850).

On the job with a caterer. You provide the guests—they do the rest. How caterers estimate party requirements; their shortcuts in food preparation; their experiences that can help the reader give better parties. Largest, most unusual assignments.

Recreation for oldsters. Survey of facilities available —and needed!—for hobbies and other recreation for retired and older folk. What civic and church groups are or should be doing. Compare with existing arrangements in other communities.

Teacher's first day on the job. What's it like to face a bunch of noisy, jumpy youngsters in a classroom for the very first time? How long does it take to remember who is Jimmy and who Johnny? What fears realized—and which not? Interview a teacher, or sit in on a class.

SEPTEMBER 3

Treaty of Paris (between England and U.S.) signed (1783) . . . New York Sun *becomes first successful penny newspaper (1833) . . . Birth of Louis Henri Sullivan (1856).*

Snakes as pets. Profile of a herpetologist, who works with (or keeps) snakes. Discussion of snakes not harmful or dangerous: their habits, diets, life expectancy. His interesting facts about snakes; breeding; other reptiles.

Training a retriever. Photos of and story about the training of gundogs—when their schooling begins, in what stages it progresses, rewards and disciplines, unusual feats.

Prize puzzlers. Interview a contestant who makes a business of participating in national contests. Prizes and cash awards won for jingles, sentence completion, other tasks. Extend to discussion of fact that these persistent puzzlers have their own publications, exchange techniques and ideas.

SEPTEMBER 4

Henry Hudson discovers Manhattan (1609) . . . Los Angeles founded (1833) . . . First self-service restaurant opens in New York (1885).

Rhythm in kids. A dancing teacher discusses the natural feeling for rhythm in many youngsters, and advises parents on best ways (games, for example) to help develop this important skill. How it helps them with music, dancing and sports.

Unusual insurance policies. An insurance company executive relates the stories of offbeat policies: a professional musician insures his hands, a stripper her natural attributes. Policies on pets; unusual floaters on prized gems and instruments; floater on a company's possessions during a move.

Rock gardens. A praise- and prize-winning gardener tells us how to go about it—shrubs, borders, Alpine plants; unusual effects for the different seasons; techniques that reduce the work of upkeep.

SEPTEMBER 5

First Continental Congress assembles (Philadelphia, 1774) . . . Standard naval uniforms adopted (1776).

Our own Romulus and Remus. We know about the founding of Rome—but who were some of the men and women responsible for cities in this state and region? Why did they make the choices they did? How arrive at the names? Did they stay on or move ahead to other places?

Seeing eye dogs. A blind master talks about his dog: describes their joint training; discusses the ways in which each guides the other; relates stories of their walks together into new sections; tells the reader what not to do when a dog and master are walking together—danger of distractions, petting, whistling.

After the hurricane. Or storm, fire or flood. A "before and after" look at a community, street, city or region. How it was before it was struck by a calamity. How it was at the peak of the disaster and immediately after. How it has been rebuilt, rehabilitated, improved. What steps have been taken to increase safety if history repeats?

SEPTEMBER 6

Pilgrims sail from Plymouth, England (1620) . . . Thomas Blanchard patents the lathe (1819) . . . Birth of Jane Addams (1860).

Rewards for baby teeth. A round-up of some of the tales and customs having to do with "prizes" left beneath the pillow when young ones lose their baby teeth.

Unusual TV effects. And how they're accomplished: storms, tiny people, talking animals, roaring space ships, other effects that tape has made possible.

"How I gave up smoking." The techniques used by a group of men and women, notables and otherwise, to rid themselves of the tobacco habit.

SEPTEMBER 7

Birth of James Fenimore Cooper (1789) . . . Death of John Greenleaf Whittier (1892) . . . Boulder (now Hoover) Dam goes into operation (1936).

Animal tracks. Show the various paw prints—can the reader identify them? An expert discusses the techniques of a master tracker.

Trade and professional associations. An insight into the activities of one of these groups, whose research and promotion efforts are so vital to the members they serve. Paid and volunteer staff. Publications. Range of activities.

How traffic accidents have been decreased at . . . . . A particular site, stretch of highway, or city. What police, traffic engineers and highway officials have done in the way of public education, new signs and signals, dividers and surveillance to prevent accidents at a place that was once a potential death trap.

SEPTEMBER 8

First Catholic parish in America organized in St. Augustine, Florida (1565) . . . Galveston hurricane and tidal wave, 5,000 die (1900).

The U. S. naval gun factory. In Washington they've made everything in weaponry from round-shot to torpedoes and rockets. From government literature and a Navy gunnery officer, build a portrait of this unusual government establishment.

Little ways in which Americans are "different." We hold the fork in one hand when cutting, in the other when carrying food to our mouth; we take salad after rather than before the main course. A European describes other little habits at the table and in public that distinguish the American.

Bargains in government surplus. The stock of a local dealer in surplus supplies—or a glance at the mail-order pages of such newspapers as the Sunday edition of The New York Times—indicates how wide is the selection and how inexpensive the prices of many no-longer-needed government supplies. A survey of what's available, for how much; the strange ends many of the items come to—parachutes become bedspreads, for example.

SEPTEMBER 9

Admission Day in California . . . William the Conqueror dies (1087) . . . Bowling rules standardized at convention of American Bowling Congress in New York (1895).

At the bank of the stream. A biologist and botanist describe the living creatures that can be found at or near the bank of a stream—from fern to tadpole, snail to frog. Photographs illustrate this picture of a microcosm.

The contents of a boy's pockets. Select a fourth- or fifth-grade class, and ask the lads to show you all the "treasures" they carry with them. You'll find the range startlingly vast. This is a fun kind of piece, and easy to extend—women's purses, men's wallets, little girls' pocketbooks, a teen-ager's top drawer.

Let's watch an actor don his make-up. Select your actor with an eye to the drama of his stage appearance—it's best if he's going to be bearded, or wigged, or if he plays the role of an aged man. Show his step-by-step progress toward the proper appearance for his role—what cosmetics he uses, the time involved, the way he alters his true appearance.

SEPTEMBER 10

First American nondenominational college chartered (Blount College, Tennessee, 1794) . . . Battle of Lake Erie (1813) . . . Birth of Charles S. Pierce (1839).

Fallout in your area. Scientists and universities and atomic energy plants and centers continuously measure the deposit rate of radioactive dust and "debris." What is the rate in your community (city, state, region)? What is the tolerable level?

What does the concertmaster do? A member of a symphonic group explains some of the terms and duties of the orchestral group—including "first" and "second" violins, "concertmaster," and so on.

"Test tube" calves. How artificial insemination is employed to improve the breed, as explained by an officer of an artificial breeding association. Dramatic changes in cattle are accomplished by this scientific method.

SEPTEMBER 11

Birth of O. Henry (1862) . . . First trackless trolley system goes into operation in Laurel Canyon, California (1910).

How old paintings are cleaned. The curator of a museum explains—or permits his restorer to be photographed as he works, thus demonstrating—the process by which old paintings are brought back to original condition. Use of modern scientific equipment (X-ray, for instance).

Poets are where you find them. And through a poetry society, you can find policemen, firemen, judges, doctors and housewives whose love is writing poetry. Portraits of these poets, samples of their work.

Radar technician. He sits at the screen in a room at the airport, or at an Army or Air Force base, or in a ship—and may act as a traffic manager, or as sentinel for a community or area. The man and his work, and an explanation of the "blips" that speak volumes to him.

SEPTEMBER 12

Defenders' Day in Maryland . . . An armored truck used in combat for first time at St. Mihiel (1918).

Initiation time on the campus. What new tortures have been discovered by collegians for new brothers, sisters and freshmen? Is this still a week when initiates prefer to eat standing at the mantel? Constructive initiation methods now supplanting the traditional "hell week."

Spirtualist tricks duplicated. A local amateur magician demonstrates and explains how "spiritualists" produce raps, tilt tables, "materialize" spirits, "read" messages, and "communicate" with the other world.

Spelling bee. Present a double column of words for members of the family to read to each other. The words should be selected from a list actually used in a national or local spelling contest for youngsters.

SEPTEMBER 13

Barry Day in Pennsylvania . . . Battle of Quebec (1759) . . . First federal election in the U.S. (1788) . . . Birth of Walter Reed (1851) . . . and John L. Pershing (1860).

"My trip to Disneyland." An as-told-to-you story, bylined by a six- or seven-year-old, recounting his or her adventures on a trip to the Disney paradise (or to Coney Island, the Mardi Gras, what have you).

Junior year abroad. A report by a college student who spent his or her third college year in a school overseas. Comparison of American and European teaching methods.

Odd bequests. Unusual gifts to your city or state (or to a college, church, or institution); gifts that came with strings attached; instances in which it was necessary to go to court to change provisions of a will.

SEPTEMBER 14

Francis Scott Key writes words to "Star-Spangled Banner" (1814) . . . Death of Aaron Burr (1836) . . . G. K. Anderson patents typewriter ribbon (1886) . . . Death of William McKinley (1901).

A forester's life. A day or week in the life of a U. S. Forest Service ranger: fire prevention, education activities, protection of visitors, use of planes in work, bombing with chemicals.

Poison control centers. Most states and cities have an emergency telephone number all parents should know—the number to call if someone swallows a toxic household product or an overdose of toxic medicine. The number—and the men, the knowledge and the emergency research resources behind that number.

If you were a TV sponsor. What would it cost to "buy time" in your city, state or region? What are the fees for talent, production, stagehands? Cost of brief station break announcements? A look at the finances of video, explained by a station manager.

SEPTEMBER 15

Birth of James Fenimore Cooper (1789) . . . Ten-hour-day labor law goes into effect in New Hampshire (1847) . . . Birth of William Howard Taft (1857).

Fines and more fines. On a given day in a given community, how much is paid in fines and to whom—for parking offenses, overdue books, traffic violations, misdemeanors, in tax penalties, and so on.

Printing the telephone directory. Almost no other publication requires such great attention to detail as the publication of a phone directory. How is the job done? Proofreading. Checking names and addresses. What happens when an error is made?

Non-public radio bands. Use of radio frequencies by taxi companies, automotive repair service stations, the police, and others who require instantaneous communication. Rules and regulations covering such use.

SEPTEMBER 16

Boston named (1630) . . . Cherokee Strip homestead rush begins (1893) . . . American Legion incorporated (1919).

Healthier teeth in a specific town. A report by dentists, health officials, parents and children on the effectiveness of a campaign for healthier teeth—whether by use of controversial fluoride additives, youth education, diet improvement, or all combined.

Remember the free lunch? An interview with a veteran bartender, and his recollections of the days when a nickel beer also gave one munching privileges. The feasts then available to quick-fingered customers.

Built-in furniture. A text-and-picture spread about ingenious built-in desks, hi-fi equipment, storage walls, base units and nursery equipment built or designed by local couples to save money and space and to give a cleaner, fresher look to their homes.

SEPTEMBER 17

Citizenship Day . . . Adoption of U.S. Constitution by delegates (1787) . . . Mercury vapor lamps patented (P. C. Hewitt, 1901).

They live their names! A lighthearted look at some local Taylors who are really tailors, Lockes in the hardware business, Knights who have dusk-to-dawn jobs, and so on.

Future Homemakers of America. This organization, founded in 1945, had more than a half-million members in its first decade. How this group for junior high schoolers—and New Homemakers for high schoolers—helps youth to contribute to better family living.

My most exciting interview. Yes—it's your turn to interview the interviewers! Their most interesting personality assignments for newspapers, magazines or television. Difficulties in arranging sessions. Personal impact of interviews.

SEPTEMBER 18

Birth of Joseph Story (1779) . . . Cornerstone of the Capitol of the U.S. laid (1793) . . . First issue of The New York Times *published (1851).*

Sobriety tests. Explanation of the teshts used by local offishers to shee if a pershon's had too much. Balloon tests, level of alcohol in bloodstream, walking a straight line. How, where employed, and with what degree of acceptability by the courts.

Reading matter from Washington. A glance at the Government Printing Office's vast publishing lists, with samples of the widely-ranging books, leaflets and periodicals available to people without charge or at minimal prices. Your representative in Washington tells about requests for literature that he receives from constituents.

Advertising in the air. From skywriting to the plane that hauls a message behind it—a story about the pilots and their business, their fees and techniques, the limitations imposed on their huckstering in the heavens by municipal and federal authorities.

SEPTEMBER 19

"I Wish I Was in Dixie" sung publicly for first time (1859) . . . Death of James A. Garfield (1881) . . . First Mickey Mouse short shown (1928).

How amateur athletes earn their living. Does their skill on the job match their ability in sports? What are their responsibilities? What unique jobs, other than typical employment as salesmen? How much time do they take from their work to participate in tournaments? Do any of the stars plan to become professionals?

American forts erected as protection against Indians. When and how they were built, and by whom. Forts that have become shrines. Battles in and around them. Life inside the forts during days of combat or siege.

Rural lighting progress. How many areas remain in county, city, state or country without full electrification? Consider such special categories as roads without electric lights, and parks and resort areas. What is the schedule for complete electrification?

SEPTEMBER 20

Ferdinand Magellan sets sail (1519) . . . American Association for the Advancement of Science organized (1848).

Assembly line in action. Most readers have a general idea of the way this factory system operates, but few of us have seen or actually worked on an assembly line. And now that further automation is underway, making this even more fascinating, describe the way the line works, depicting each job stage, time permitted for each operation, safeguards against inaccuracy and error.

A celebrity's baby-memory book. When a young person in your environs achieves fame as an athlete, entertainer or scholar, do a different interview—by going over with him and his parents his baby-memory book or snapshot collection, and using these photos as your illustrations.

Counter jargon. Almost anyone can decipher *some* of the shouted instructions to a short-order cook. ("Crack two broken" or "burn one" could, in some areas, mean "two fried eggs" or "one order of toast.") But what of some of the other shortcuts?

SEPTEMBER 21

Birth of Louis Jolliet (1645) and H. G. Wells (1866) . . . Duryea Motor Wagon Company incorporated (1895).

Blood bank. Dramatize the operation of this vital community service by "tracing" a pint of plasma from donor to patient. Are sufficient blood contributions being received? Are certain blood types now in greatest need? How is blood treated and stored?

He's building his own boat. Small boats are being made in backyards for fun and profit—and your story pictures a man doing just this, showing how his family pitches in, how he fits this project into his busy week, his schedule of operations from planning to the great day of launching the craft.

"My first job." Interviews with celebrities or municipal officials (or company presidents, etc.) about their first paid labors; humorous experiences on the job. Did they set their sights for the future on the basis of this youthful work?

SEPTEMBER 22

Nathan Hale hanged (1776) . . . Birth of Michael Faraday (1791) . . . First U.S. business high school opens in Washington, D.C. (1890).

Burns and scalds. First-aid advice from a health official or physician for management and relief of minor burns. In the event of major burns—what to do until the ambulance arrives.

Management consultant. A new kind of expert in the business community—the consultant who moves from problem to problem in many different companies. A profile of this man (or organization) and his methods; success stories; personal background.

Cake decorators supreme. The talents of a skilled housewife and a professional baker compared—and what each can teach the other in creative cake decoration . . . from buttercream flowers to fancy lettering.

SEPTEMBER 23

Battle of Bonhomme Richard *and* Serapis *(1779) . . . Birth of William Holmes McGuffey (1800) . . . Lewis and Clark reach St. Louis (1806).*

Make a mobile! An artist explains how to make one of these ever-moving, ever-changing miracles of art, balance and design. Photographic illustrations plus text guide the do-it-yourself reader.

Shopping for a zoo. The "shopping list" of meats, vegetables and fish required to feed the inhabitants of a specific zoölogical garden. Unusual delicacies that must be obtained for the daily diet of some of the more exotic creatures. Where supplies are purchased, and how frequently. Vitamin supplements, too?

Chalk-talk fun. A blackboard artist who entertains at churches and schools shows some of his witty crayon tricks, describes the way he adds to his fund of stunts, comments on his audiences and their reactions.

SEPTEMBER 24

Birth of John Marshall (1755) . . . Office of the Attorney General created (1789) . . . Birth of Marcus Hanna (1837).

Overseas secretary. Many government jobs are available for the stenographer and typist who can go abroad. A civil service official can explain the requirements for such a post and the many rewards it carries with it.

Those deposit bottles. How are they washed and checked? What percentage of bottles are broken, chipped, or otherwise put out of service? What's the average life of a deposit bottle?

Appreciating an art masterpiece. The head of an art department analyzes a famous painting and explains just what it is that makes this work immortal. Movement, color, dramatic effect, balance, depth, perspective—all these discussed for the lay reader.

SEPTEMBER 25

Balboa discovers Pacific (1513) . . . First major U.S. bank robbery (National Bank, Concord, Massachusetts, 1865) . . . Birth of William Faulkner (1897).

The traveling "ham." Many radio amateurs are now going "mobile"—and the facts of portable radio reception and transmission are outlined here by one such "ham." He also covers special regulations, discusses his equipment, reveals the special thrills of his hobby.

Junior satellite experts. At the junior high and high schools of your area, there are sure to be bands of young scientists who are making and launching rockets. Interviews, the story of how they do it, successes, their own innovations, their space ambitions.

Shadowgraph artist. He waves his hands and manipulates his fingers in front of a beam of light—and on the silver screen you see birds, animals, pugilists. Photos of his hands—and the silhouettes the audience sees. How he learned this entertaining art.

SEPTEMBER 26

British occupy Philadelphia (1777) . . . Death of Daniel Boone (1820) . . . Birth of George Gershwin (1898) . . . Federal Trade Commission organized (1914).

Country editor. He's the all-around man of journalism, a community force, adviser to many—and a job-printer on the side. The 36-hour-a-day life of the small-town editor, the rewards and worries, his poignant and his laugh-provoking experiences.

"Questions about kids." A veteran pediatrician recalls for you the questions he's invariably asked by new parents. And then he tries to answer them, once and for all!

Whittlers. Fifty or more years ago, any group of men would not be found just talking—but whittling as well. A veteran whittler proudly displays some of his more intricate works, the wood and knife he uses, and tells why his hobby seems to be a dying art.

SEPTEMBER 27

Birth of Samuel Adams (1722) . . . First steam-locomotive for railroad put in use (England, 1825).

An educational TV station. The operations of a non-commercial station, and the information and guidance it provides for youngsters, professionals, and teachers in the community, along with programs of more than educational impact.

National Park holiday. A family's own story of their trip to one or more of the nation's magnificent park systems—illustrated, naturally, with the family's own snapshots, comments on the budget, supplies they took or wished they had taken with them.

Offbeat hospitals. Doll hospitals—and "hospitals" for shirts, watches, pets, toys, and so on. How the "patients" are "cured."

SEPTEMBER 28

New York City imports its first fireboat (from England, 1800) . . . Birth of Thomas Nast (1840) . . . First round-the-world flight ends successfully in Seattle (time: 175 days —about 350 hours of them in air—begun April 6, 1924, ended this day in 1924).

Operating a reservoir. Not only its functions of water supply and purification, and not only the testing and scientific methodology of these functions—but the resort aspects for campers, hunters, sailors, and vacationers at national reservoirs.

Planning and building a golf course. The good Lord may have made the hills, but He didn't add the sand traps and artificial water traps. A member of the National Golf Foundation explains how those 18 holes are carefully planned to produce the correct balance of fun and torture.

Gospel recordings. Each year the sale of these records increases dramatically. Which singers are most popular in your city, state or region? Which records are perennial bestsellers? Report from a record distributor or one of the artists.

SEPTEMBER 29

Birth of Lord Nelson (1758) . . . First night football game (Mansfield, Pennsylvania, 1892) . . . Death of Winslow Homer (1910).

Watching a rumor spread. To demonstrate the incredible swiftness with which rumor or gossip sweeps a group, try (with permission!) an experiment. For example, idly mention to a school youngster that you "heard" that there was going to be a special test for all kids later that day. Then your story charts the way the rumor travels and increases itself.

Tugboats. A day on one of the tough and powerful little odd-jobber and general handyman vessels of river and harbor. The crew, and their duties; rescue and salvage operations; towing; steering large ships to the dock.

"The habit I'd like to break." Notables confess that they'd like to stop cussing, smoking, eating candy, cracking knuckles, pulling at ear-lobes—no need to list more, is there?

SEPTEMBER 30

First execution for murder in America—John Billington (1630), one of the signers of the Plymouth Compact.

House organ editor. There's a vast circulation for the "internal" and "external" publications issued by business and industry—and an association of "house organ" editors who can supply insight into the special goals and efforts of these company magazines and newspapers.

Indian souvenirs—where do they come from? An amusing article can be based on the fact that "authentic souvenirs" you purchase at Indian reservations (or a number of similar tourist shops) come from Japan, Germany, other sections of the country—and are machine made, moreover!

How to ask for a raise. Interview men from top management to find how they react to the usual requests for a raise they receive. What kind of request or demand do they lightly dismiss with an excuse? And which bring about the desired results?

OCTOBER 1

First city directory published (Philadelphia, 1785) . . . First baseball World Series (1903) . . . Model-T Ford introduced (1908).

Lost arts. The making of stained-glass windows, for example, or certain forms of enamel work. These are just two arts practiced centuries ago that modern man cannot truly duplicate. And the curator of a museum, an archeologist, or a professor of the arts can describe many more.

Work-and-study colleges. An increasing number of colleges are now adopting the "six weeks of work, six weeks of study" approach—with reasons that are both economical and psychological. An insight into one such college. (A high-school guidance counselor in your community can supply basic information.)

The wonders of modern wood. For one thing, many laminated woods prove stronger and more durable in fires than metal! The strength, varieties, ease in use and adaptability of modern woods, as explained by an architect or builder.

OCTOBER 2

Missouri Day . . . Death of Samuel Adams (1803) . . . Patent given to J. Osterhoudt for tin can to be opened with key (1866) . . . Johns Hopkins University opened (1876).

Taxes add up! Show how much of the money an average person might spend in one full day goes for sales taxes, gasoline and liquor taxes, entertainment and communications taxes—and so on!

Literary forgeries. A dealer in rare books, letters and autographs will regale you with tales of bibliographic frauds and forgeries. Odds are that he has been stung once or twice himself!

Behind Little League baseball. The team may be small in stature or size—but behind it you'll find a crowd of supporters, backers, coaches and aides. Show the people, the companies, the groups, the intensive adult effort that is poured into just one team.

OCTOBER 3

Death of Miles Standish (1656) . . . First engineering college (Rensselaer Polytechnic Institute) founded (Troy, New York, 1824).

How long does it take? To become a nurse, a lawyer, a psychoanalyst, an airlines pilot, a licensed barber, a Ph.D.? Careers—and the investments of time and money required to get to the point where one can begin!

Little ways to lengthen life. A nap after dinner . . . a daily walk . . . a slight change in diet . . . a better breakfast—these are some of the minor things that can be done by adults to make their lives longer and healthier. A health department official lists such suggestions, and explains how they'll help.

The honor system works! Show in how many ways the citizen of your community or city has a daily chance to prove (or disprove) his honesty. Newspapers taken from racks where there are coin boxes, not a newsdealer or newsboy . . . examinations at schools . . . the list is longer than you think!

OCTOBER 4

*Feast of St. Francis of Assissi (1182) . . .
Birth of Rutherford B. Hayes (1822) . . .
First power press for printing fine books patented by Isaac Adams (1830).*

If you wanted to change your name. Think of the unhappy few Americans whose name was Hitler! Suppose *you* want a new last name: what must be done? How long does it take? Any costs involved? From the same judge who gives you this information, you can probably winnow a number of name-changing anecdotes.

The symbolism of numbers. Why is "13" considered an unlucky number? Or "7," on the other hand, a lucky figure? A mathematics expert can reveal many fascinating facts about beliefs in the occult and mystic virtues and powers of numbers, and about numerology as a whole.

What makes secretaries mad. The girls themselves—anonymously, of course!—describe the ways in which bosses drive them to tears or rage. Some sample sins—beginning dictation at 4:50 P.M.; insisting that a particular assignment is a rush job, and then, when it's done, putting it aside; and asking poor steno to do wife's shopping!

OCTOBER 5

Birth of Jonathan Edwards (1703) and Chester Alan Arthur (1830). . . . Nation's first baby show, Springfield, Ohio (1854) . . . Birth of Pablo Picasso (1881).

"The day I'll never forget." A group of notables remember, for example, the day Pearl Harbor was bombed . . . or when F.D.R. died . . . or the day of a blizzard . . . or a red-letter day in their own personal history.

Operations of a magazine wholesaler. He distributes a multitude of weekly and monthly periodicals to newsstands . . . and keeps the racks filled with paper-bound books . . . and then picks up unsold copies and adds to the stock of the fast-selling publications. How does his staff operate? What's his warehouse like? (He's also the man who knows what people are reading—and whether they're reading more.)

Language records—for the birds! If you want to teach your parrot, budgerigar or parakeet to "talk" —you can buy a record that will help do the job. Describe these very special disks and assess their effectiveness. (Is there also a record that teaches the bird when to be quiet?)

OCTOBER 6

First Turkish Bath opens in New York City (1863).

Plate? Sterling? Sheffield? What are the differences in these various forms of silver? What are the distinctions in beauty, durability, cost? A jeweler explains in detail and adds tips on the care of silver.

"My aching back!" An orthopedist explains why so many of us do have back problems. Poor posture, high heels and incorrect lifting are a few of the causes. What to do, what not to do. Helpful exercises. Mattresses. How to sit.

Phones in cars. Thousands of Americans can now chat by phone while waiting for the light to change or the traffic jam to ease. A telephone company executive discusses costs, installation, statistics of carphones in your region, who uses them and why.

OCTOBER 7

Stamp Act Congress opens (1765) . . . Birth of James Whitcomb Riley (1777) . . . Death of Oliver Wendell Holmes (1894) . . . Full-size electric starting gates used at race track for first time (San Francisco, 1939).

Danger! Man loose in supermarket! Stand at a check-out counter when the men puff up pushing a wagon-load of items their wives didn't want. Find out why men are the "impulse buyers." Does the wife ever return hubby's purchases the following day?

Word games. First there was "Ghost" and then "Super-Ghost." And from members of an English department you'll find many more word and letter games to pass on to your readers. Samples and instructions.

Under the city streets. There's a network of cables, pipes, sewers! How records are kept of this tangle of vital arteries; the responsibility for upkeep; safeguards while repairing. Describe one area of maximum underground concentration.

OCTOBER 8

Chicago Fire starts (1871) . . . First Vanderbilt Cup Race (Hicksville, Long Island, 1904) . . . Alvin York's incredible feat (1918).

Local "Johnny Appleseeds." Profile of an individual who is particularly devoted to trees; who, for example, has spearheaded a movement to line streets or highways with elm, maple, or weeping willow. Leaders who attempt to funnel public opinion into reforestation or conservation programs.

Absolute pitch. A musician discusses the perfect "musical ear," describing how students practice recognition of notes by taking musical dictation. Examples of musicians and conductors able to detect tiniest variations.

Old enough to vote? A pre-election-period survey of opinions by adolescents, parents, teachers and political leaders on whether the voting age should be lowered. Discussion of variations across country.

OCTOBER 9

Leif Ericson Day . . . Founding of Yale College (1701) . . . International Association for Criminal Identification (through fingerprints) formed (Oakland, California, 1915).

The audience for foreign films. "Art films" are the newest force in movie entertainment. What about in your city, state or region? What does the exhibitor think about the trend—will it last, influence American-made movies, break down censorship or taboos?

A richer social life for the handicapped. Your local association for retarded, palsied or mute children describes the efforts being made to provide more fun, companionship and social growth for these youngsters and young adults. How other groups help them. What is still needed. Volunteer workers—on the job or being sought.

Guarding a department store. All the steps taken, day and night, to prevent looting or pilfering—from night watchmen accompanied by trained watchdogs to mirror systems, department store detectives, watchful clerks.

OCTOBER 10

U.S. Naval Academy opens (1845) . . . Ivory-like billiard ball patented by J. W. Hyatt (1865) . . . Birth of Helen Hayes (1900).

Our expanding junior colleges. Portrait of the growth of the two-year college—locally and nationally, as narrated by the president or dean of such an institution. Courses, students, campus life, transfers to full colleges, degrees, specialties—a full picture of goals and facilities.

Preventing back-seat bedlam. Tips on traveling with kids—games to play, songs to sing, contests; what to carry in a back-seat basket.

Caring for the convalescent. A nurse tells us what we ought to know about keeping a patient just back from the hospital as happy and comfortable as possible.

OCTOBER 11

Pulaski Memorial Day (he died in 1799) . . . First steam ferry in operation (New York-Hoboken, 1811) . . . Birth of Eleanor Roosevelt (1884).

Sales manager at work. Profile of the man responsible for a network of salesmen. How he inspires them with contests, bulletins, leads; his problems with the "swindle sheet"; his notions about changing sales conditions; his star salesman.

Marine shells. A collector discusses the vast variety of shells to be found on the beaches she has visited; is pictured with her prizes; discusses the "market" for shells; tells how and why she began collecting.

Adding sound to home movies. The newest wrinkle for camera hobbyists is the addition of dialogue, commentary, music, and amusing sound effects. An expert tells how it's done, with what equipment, and describes his proudest achievements. Your camera store can lead you to him.

OCTOBER 12

Columbus Day . . . Birth of John Hay (1838) . . . Death of Robert E. Lee (1870) . . . First official amateur golf tournament held in Newport, Rhode Island (1895).

The toughest job on the eleven. The quarterback's role, as related by a football coach. His job of strategy, signals, leadership, turning disadvantages into assets. Training procedures of the coach. His list of great quarterbacks.

Lightning. What it really is, how it is generated in nature (and science!), freak lightning accidents, preventing lightning damage.

Solitaire. One-handed card games described and explained, along with cautions about cheating oneself!

OCTOBER 13

Cornerstone of Executive Mansion laid in Washington, D.C. (1792) . . . First aerial photograph made (from a balloon in Boston, 1860).

A textbook depository. Interview the person in charge of the mountains of textbooks distributed to the students of a county. How many textbooks are on hand, and are many replaced because of wear and tear? How often are textbooks changed by the board of education?

Row, row, row your boat! Interview the owner or operator of a public rowboat concession. How he keeps his crafts shipshape. Unusual boats in public parks—swan boats, pedal boats, ice boats. Are sailors on leave really his best customers? What about gallantry afloat—or does hubby insist that the wife pull her own oars?

How to make your tires last longer. The proprietor of a tire shop offers hints toward longer tire life. Under-and-over-inflation. Bruise dangers. Handling a skidding car. Blowouts. New developments in patches and plugs. Rigorous tests for development of new tires.

OCTOBER 14

Battle of Hastings (1066) . . . Birth of William Penn (1644) . . . George Eastman receives patent for transparent paper strip photographic film (1884) . . . Birth of Dwight D. Eisenhower (1890).

Eye examinations for pre-schoolers. If the children can't read, what substitutes are used for those diminishing letters on the chart? (Answer: such things as pictures of lollipops, dogs, balls!) Other devices to test the sight of infants and toddlers.

Junior League president. The philanthropic, community and social activities of this busy and extensive group. Achievements during the past year. Goals for the future. A profile of the busy lady who coördinates all these projects.

How it feels to sell door-to-door. Arm yourself with a product that sells for a quarter and try to sell it for a nickel by ringing doorbells. Experiences with the suspicious, talkative, angry, friendly, disinterested or delighted matrons met in the course of the day.

OCTOBER 15

Poetry Day . . . Edison Electric Light Company incorporated in New York (1878) . . . Mata Hari (Gertrud Margarete Zelle) executed in 1917.

They make their own greeting cards. Samples of the work of people who make woodcuts, linoleum-block prints, photographic cards—and send truly personal greeting cards to their friends.

What you'd earn if. . . . you were a typical physician, barber, pilot, stewardess, supermarket clerk, insurance salesman, and so on. A survey of earnings and earning potential in a variety of trades and professions.

Artillery salutes. From a "five-gun salute" for a vice-consul to twenty-one for a vice-president. An artillery officer explains the custom of salutes, ruffles and flourishes, and appropriate music. Tie in with visits by dignitaries to a camp, base or community.

OCTOBER 16

Birth of Noah Webster (1758) and Oscar Wilde (1854) . . . John Brown's raid (1859) . . . Birth of Eugene O'Neill (1888) . . . First student enrolled by International Correspondence School (1891).

Turkey-farm facts. The new breeds being developed; the Thanksgiving-centered calendar of operation; strange habits of the turkeys (fear of strangers, panic in the pens); favorite recipes. Preparations for the big day just a few weeks hence.

Personnel agency. The director of an agency explains how he finds jobs for applicants and applicants for jobs. How the applicant can make a good first impression on the potential employer. How to write a good resumé.

Page boy in Congress. An interview with one of the lads who serves as a small but significant cog in the legislative machinery. His working hours, social life, schooling; comments about legislators; his personal political ambitions.

OCTOBER 17

General Burgoyne surrenders (1777) . . . Al Capone convicted of income-tax evasion, sentenced to prison (1931).

Cafe expresso. Going fancy with the coffee bean has become a thriving business. In every big city there are now "coffee houses" that are part European in tradition (i.e., chess sets and literary magazines available) and part American (i.e., juke boxes, albeit with classics and folk-songs). Your lead, however, might be recipes from restaurants—for Irish coffee, the Viennese brew, and other exotic cups.

An interview with the chaplain of a college. His activities; the percentage of students who are church members. The chaplain's comments about youth and religion. Chapel exercises. Religious facilities for students of other denominations. Counseling.

Conelrad. A civil defense official and a radio station manager explain this system, and its role in instructing the public on two kinds of attack: by the forces of nature and by an enemy. How, in the event of war, the Conelrad system will make it less likely that the enemy can issue false radio news and instructions.

OCTOBER 18

S. F. B. Morse lays first cable (1842) . . . Alaska Day (1859), transfer of territory from Russia to U.S. . . . Death of Thomas Alva Edison (1931).

What you should know about contracts. Laymen often sign an agreement without realizing that they've signed a binding contract; and frequently, these contracts guarantee nothing except grief. Ask a representative of the Better Business Bureau, a Legal Aid Society, or the district attorney's office to explain and, most of all, warn against hasty signatures.

Laboratory animals. The care and breeding of the rodents, simians, and other animals used to help scientists save human lives. Methods to prevent infection among animals, confusion, extraneous disorders. Difficulties in obtaining certain species that are imported. Occasional use of such groups as Boy Scouts to collect needed insects, toads, and other laboratory creatures.

Big business helps colleges. A survey of the considerable sums given by industry to institutions of higher education. Funds for research, in the form of scholarships and fellowships; endowments; use of facilities; donation of equipment; salary increments for faculty.

OCTOBER 19

Birth of John Adams (1735) . . . Cornwallis surrenders at Yorktown (1781) . . . There's a wedding in a balloon above Cincinnati, Ohio (1874), a "first."

Blind dates. Using local or national notables—or, for other markets, perhaps the members of one sorority and one fraternity—get personal-experience anecdotes about arranged dates; attitude toward them by girls and young men; blind dates that led to engagement and marriage.

Detention homes. Should they be eliminated or drastically changed? Some authorities insist that these "shelters" for young people involved in crime only serve to breed further antisocial habits. Others claim that detention homes are necessary. Profile of a home, with controversial statements about it.

Doll clothes. A number of hobbyists specialize in "socks"—the late 19th century dolls made from socks and lavishly, authentically dressed. And then there's the big field of people interested in doll clothes of the 1860's. Interviews with collectors; photographs; facts about this hobby.

OCTOBER 20

Mount Union College founded to give women absolutely equal rights with male students (1846) . . . Birth of John Dewey (1859).

Would anyone know where to look? Address that question to your reader. In case of an emergency, would his family know where to find his insurance papers, will, financial records? Bankers or surrogates can list the information needed by survivors or by a family when illness strikes, and will suggest a family checklist.

Temper, temper! A round-up of examples of dramatic displays of temperament. The bus driver who deserted his vehicle and passengers, the well-known golfer who *did* break his clubs—examples of this make an amusing feature. Comments by a psychologist would be instructive.

Wives who have gone back to work. Now that the children are at school or are married, these wives have returned to their businesses, trades or professions. Interview a cross-section for the problems and rewards of such later-years employment.

OCTOBER 21

Birth of Samuel T. Coleridge (1772) . . . Lord Nelson defeats French and Spanish fleets (1805) . . . Reserve Officer Training Corps established (1916).

Family medical records. A physician explains what information we should keep at hand about past illnesses, X-ray therapy, vaccinations and inoculations, illnesses of parents and grandparents, allergies to foods and drugs, and so on. With dramatic case histories, demonstrate that such information (sometimes forgotten during emergencies) can save lives.

Dog discipline. First night at a class where dogs learn to heel, stay, halt at intersections, and act like gentlemen when walking on a street. The trainer and his methods. Advanced groups.

Filmstrips in schools. Sources and subjects of the many teaching aids in "slide" or filmstrip form used at all levels of our schools. Teacher and student appraisal. Methods of tying-in with curriculum and textbooks. Filmstrips with accompanying records.

OCTOBER 22

Princeton University (then College of New Jersey) chartered (1746) . . . Birth of Franz Liszt (1811) . . . First national horse show opens (New York City, 1883).

Fire drill at home. Suppose fire broke out suddenly one night in your bedroom or kitchen—how would your family escape? What would you try to save? Fire officials urge occasional "at home" fire drills so that tots and adults know just what to do.

Flowers by wire. How does this system work? Your local florist and the state association of florists will describe their network of participating stores, their high standards, methods used to communicate complex orders quickly.

Odd names of cafes. Check phone directories, cafe owners, travelers for unusual names they have seen in various states. Is "Busy Bee" really common? Are the most elegant appellations found over some of the most dreadful eateries?

OCTOBER 23

Birth of Sarah Bernhardt (1845) . . . Bryn Mawr opens as first graduate college for women (1885).

A multipurpose garage. Using local or regional examples, show how homeowners are now building play areas, workshop facilities, guest quarters, and home offices into renovated or new garages. Build-it-yourself information based on these actual de luxe garages.

Ghost stories. In preparation for Halloween, assemble a group of ghost stories in brief that once terrified a specific group of people—celebrities, say, or police officers.

Oddity expert. Profile of a collector of odd facts—the believe-it-or-not-type—concerning a community, the state, or some other subject. Is this a hobby or a money-making vocation? His best sources of material; checking the stories.

OCTOBER 24

United Nations Day . . . Seth Thomas patents his one-day, back-wind alarm clock (1876) . . . George Washington Bridge opens for traffic (New York, 1931).

Letters sent and received by the First Lady of your state. Does the governor's wife correspond with a number of shut-ins? Describe one day's typical mail —crank epistles; requests for money; letters seeking advice on romantic or business affairs; invitations; comments on political matters; requests to serve on committees. Slant: The First Lady's service through letters.

Grading of meat. What do those stamps mean? Why the different shapes and colors of the inspector's markings? What are the differences between "prime," "choice," and "good"? What stamps should one watch out for? A U. S. Department of Agriculture authority explains.

When to call an ambulance. Some symptoms of sudden illness are "red flags" that should send you speeding to the phone for emergency help. A doctor explains what they are and what you should do (and *not* do) until help arrives.

OCTOBER 25

St. Crispin's Day . . . Battle of Agincourt (1415) . . . The Charge of the Light Brigade (1854) . . . Birth of Richard E. Byrd (1888).

City attorney. What are the jobs of a city attorney? Typical legal headaches encountered during his term. Show difficulties in zoning decisions, purchases, suits against the municipality, special problems encountered in advice to schools, hospitals, etc.

Teen-age fads. What are the latest "rages" in slang, fashion accessories, hair styles, dances, entertainers, foods, parties, and "pinning" among high-schoolers?

Fair employment practices committee. A unit in your city or state concerned with eliminating bias in hiring. Cases in which religious or racial prejudice were affecting employment, and how this committee was able to put an end to it.

OCTOBER 26

Erie Canal opened for traffic (1825) . . . First jacks in U. S. were sent to George Washington by Charles III of Spain on this day—which is how breeding of mules began (1785) . . . Death of Elizabeth Cady Stanton (1902).

One-room schools. Are there any left in your state or region? Reminiscences by a school principal who began his career as a teacher in a "little red schoolhouse." Portrait of such a school if you can locate one.

What they won't make into lamps! Pictures of odd items used as lamp bases—old telephones, wine bottles, driftwood, candy jars, pistols, textile-design rollers, and so on.

The activities of a lecture bureau. Behind those platform appearances is the matter of poring over maps, timetables, air schedules, and hotel rates. Biggest names in the lecture field; lecturers who make use of motion pictures; do the speakers find that the questioning period for the audience is largely repetitive, city to city?

OCTOBER 27

Navy Day (to celebrate birth of Theodore Roosevelt in 1858) . . . First New York subway opens (1904).

Student elections. Report on the race for student president at a particular school. Show campaign posters, slogans, words of songs. The "platform" of the competing nominees. Counting the vote.

Saying "Grace." The favorite prayers recited at the table by ministers, church officials, notables.

Opinion polls. Accompany a researcher on his or her expedition in search of facts and opinions. Techniques used by the questioner. How opinion researchers are paid. Is this a good source of part-time income? Research on the campus and in the supermarket. Those telephone checks on programs.

OCTOBER 28

Founding of Harvard College (1636) . . . Statue of Liberty dedicated (1886) . . . St. Louis adopts fingerprinting system (1904).

Remember those penmanship exercises? The circles, loops, and lines we used to practice as part of the Spencerian system. What penmanship exercises are employed in elementary schools today?

"Do you like your given name?" The answers of city and county officials. How some of the officials received their names. Favorite names. Little-known middle names of officials.

Photographic surveying. Cameras used in this type of work; number of photographs taken in an average survey; advantages of this method of surveying.

OCTOBER 29

Sir Walter Raleigh executed (1618) . . . Birth of James Boswell (1740) and John Keats (1795) . . . "Black Tuesday" at New York Stock Exchange (1929).

An antique car enthusiast. The oldest automobile in his collection; unique machines; the cars most difficult to obtain. The problem of keeping the "horseless carriages" in running condition; speeds attained by the various automobiles; the dollar value of the collection. Visitors; correspondence; his wife's attitude.

Neurosis? psychosis? complex? A psychiatrist defines these terms for laymen, along with a discussion of the differences between various types of psychologist, psychiatrist, analyst, and so on.

"Night in . . ." What happens in a given community when night approaches. A thorough survey of changing loads on utilities companies, transportation services, activities of such municipal protection groups as police and firemen, downtown traffic, hustle and bustle around amusement areas, commuter traffic, and so on.

OCTOBER 30

Birth of William Graham Sumner (1840) . . . Orson Welles' famous "invasion" program (1938).

Conscience money. How persons send sums to city, county, and state treasurers to salve their consciences in connection with thefts, evasion of taxes, etc. Conscience funds spanning considerable periods, amounting to large sums or very small amounts.

Campus gardener. What's involved in keeping a vast college campus beautiful—cultivating grass, maintaining shrubbery, tree surgery, etc. Special problems caused by student activities.

"My first circus." Description by residents of your city of their earliest contacts with the Big Top—the clowns' pranks, animals, stunts, and the thrill of watching a circus unload at dawn. Do any of the oldsters still attend circus performances?

OCTOBER 31

Halloween . . . Nevada Day . . . Martin Luther nails theses against abuses to Castle Church door (1517).

Pets in stores. Have any animals gone on rampages, like the proverbial bull in a china shop? What are typical municipal regulations about pets in shops and restaurants? How a manager can handle such a situation without raising a scene.

Make vacation plans now! How to obtain tour information from gasoline companies, automobile clubs, chambers of commerce, hotel and motel associations, railroads, airlines, and so on. The need for early reservations in state and federal park areas.

Laundry marks that trap the criminal. Murders and other crimes solved by such marks. Using ultraviolet lamps to detect invisible laundry marks. Identification through such markings. Slant: "You're a marked man!"

NOVEMBER 1

Liberty Day in the Virgin Islands . . . The Stamp Act goes into effect (1765) . . . Texas proclaims independence from Mexico (1835) . . . Boston Female Medical School —first for women—organized (1848) . . . Birth of Stephen Crane (1871).

Experimental designs. A round-up of what a number of products are expected to look like a decade from now—automobiles, kitchen appliances, plumbing equipment, telephones, pleasure boats, and so on. Large companies and package designers will supply both photographs and details.

Speed up your reading! Reading clinics, private or associated with colleges or high schools, use a number of dramatic techniques to teach people how to read up to a thousand words a minute! The story of a clinic; the values of faster, more incisive reading; methods; students; a reading test.

Foster home care. A story, proceeding from the local scene to the state, regional or national situation, depicting the demand for foster homes. Go inside the home of a family that has taken a foster child to it—showing joys, for child and foster family; discussion of finances; problems of the foster child; qualifications of the foster parents.

NOVEMBER 2

Birth of Daniel Boone (1734), James K. Polk (1795), Warren G. Harding (1865).

Snow removal methods. New equipment for home-owner and community that will help beat the problems of snow and ice this winter. Discuss chemicals that promote melting; home power equipment and attachments. Sidewalk heating; giant new plows that not only clear a path but grind snow and ice; and—as a last resort—community plans for hiring shovelers.

A pediatrician's advice to grandparents. Baby John and little Mary can be helped by Grandma and Grandpa to a life of more fun and knowledge—or their grandparents can confuse them, spoil them, contradict the parent's wishes and instructions. A pediatrician tells grandparents and prospective grandparents somc of his experiences, both good and bad, and offers a checklist against which they can judge themselves.

Greeting card verse. Has the trend toward "sick" humor and one-line jokes on cards diminished the market for verse? How do the manufacturers acquire the ideas and copy? A local writer of such material describes the market, its needs, the rate of payment.

NOVEMBER 3

Panama Independence Day . . . Birth of Stephen Austin (1793) and William Cullen Bryant (1794) . . . WCTU organized (1883).

Wig-maker. While the toupee continues to cover the male market, so to speak, colorful wigs for women have actually become "high fashion." A specialist in hair pieces describes his art, showing steps in the preparation of a wig or toupee.

How crowded are our classrooms? Proceeding from the local situation up through city, state and region, survey the actual number of children in classes vs. the ideal, the ratio of teachers to students, facilities that are and should be available, the number of schools that must run shortened "split sessions" to accommodate pupil load, plans for the increasing rush of school-age youngsters.

Ice sculpture. You'll find statues and structures made of ice in the banquet hall, created by chefs—and on the campus, fashioned by collegians. And in the backyard or on the school grounds, snow sculptors create other ephemeral masterpieces. A photo-grapic survey of some of these creations, with much of your story devoted to the individual or gang at work on one particular ice statue.

NOVEMBER 4

Patent for artificial leg granted to B. F. Palmer (1846) . . . Birth of Will Rogers (1879).

Education and earnings. Educators say that over a period of thirty years, a college education is worth at least $100,000 in extra earnings. A clerk with a high-school degree may earn $4,000 a year—American physicians average $23,000 annually. Discuss with educators and personnel directors to demonstrate the importance of education from this "breadwinner" point of view.

It won't hurt a bit! New devices used by the dentist to reduce pain caused by drilling, cleaning, extractions. Some of his new equipment is electronic, with the work performed by high-frequency soundwaves.

The story behind a cruise. When a ship sets sail for a several-weeks' voyage, it must be ready to serve as hotel and amusement park—and must have provisions for care of the ill, for supervision of children, for housing of pets. Present the statistics behind this pleasure voyage—supplies of food, liquor, linens, the commissary; the size of the crew; the duties and responsibilities of the bursar, entertainment director, chief chef, and so on.

NOVEMBER 5

Guy Fawkes Day . . . First colonial post office established (Massachusetts, 1639) . . . American Society of Civil Engineers founded (1852) . . . Birth of Eugene Victor Debs (1855).

It sprays! The vast expansion of the aerosol bomb industry, as seen in the grocery, the pharmacy, the hardware store, the art supply shop, at the cosmetic counter, and so on. Odd items now found in these pressure cans—rubber cement, dentifrices, and so on. By the way—does disposal of this array of bombs present new problems for the municipal sanitation force?

Soldiers abroad. Now that it's time to start mailing Christmas packages abroad, a story is timely (on the local, regional or national level) covering the number of men in our armed forces stationed overseas. Where they are, how long they are assigned to this foreign duty, frequency of furloughs home, gifts especially welcomed abroad.

Sir, that's slander! What the ordinary person may think of as gossip or as justifiable, angry denunciation—can be considered slander by a judge, and can result in serious penalties. A lawyer or magistrate discusses this little-known but vital subject.

NOVEMBER 6

Birth of John Phillip Sousa (1854) . . . First intercollegiate football game (Rutgers vs. Princeton, 1869).

New ways in wallpapering. Now even a one-armed person can do it! A decorator or supplier of wallpapers explains how new adhesives, along with other advances in packaging and pre-preparation of the papers, make it possible for the "do-it-yourself" fan to do a quick, capable job. You can accompany with photographs of an actual job, from start to finish.

"The electric eye is on you." When you walk through the door at supermarket or terminal . . . or pull up at the window of a drive-in bank . . . or set your luggage on the proper conveyor at the airport . . . or drive up to many garages—the electric eye is focused on you and is ready to act as servant or sleuth. A survey of the many uses of this device in one community.

Experiments with E.S.P. Perform your own experiments in your own community with the cards used to test and measure the degree of extrasensory perception in individuals. Use several "categories"—e.g., school children, detectives, housewives.

NOVEMBER 7

Birth of Marie Curie (1867) . . . Jeannette Rankin is first woman elected as a U.S. Representative (1916) . . . Russian Revolution begins (1917).

How a mutual fund works. Millions of Americans are now investing in this new, "co-op" way—hoping, for the most part, to decrease risks by spreading their investment over many different stocks. The manager of a fund explains its operations, the "installment method" of participation, the statistics of mutual funds in the U.S. today.

On the road with a show. Pity the man in charge of taking a Broadway hit on tour! He must worry about scenery, lighting, dressing-room facilities, ticket sales, promotion, advertising, transportation for the cast, hotel reservations, luggage, first-aid emergencies, temperament—and much, much more. Interview this harried individual for an insight into his extraordinarily complicated mission.

Riddles. Ask a group of children one riddle—and you'll get dozens in return. At a certain pre-teen-age level, this is the favorite form of wit. (And educators say that it shows a healthy interest in words and meanings.) Your story, of course, should include many sample sticklers.

NOVEMBER 8

The Louvre opens (1793) . . . First ferry exclusively for cars and their passengers goes into service between Weehawken, New Jersey, and New York City (1926) . . . North African invasion begins (1942).

Meteorites falling! In museums and at some meteorological stations, you can view meteorites that have fallen in your region—and from experts at these centers, you can learn more about the way the earth has been showered, over the years, by these astonishing objects. The how's and why's of meteorites.

Fad diets. A physician or nutritionist will tell you about the unusual diets adopted by folks in search of slimness—nine oranges a day, nothing but bananas, steak and black coffee, etc.—and why (although they may work) they are dangerous in most cases. A discussion of saner approaches to a better shape.

Watching war games. At many Army camps, there's a once-a-year battle that has its full quota of mock casualties, "prisoners," landings, tank attacks, espionage—even air cover and paratrooper drops. Describe your service as a "war correspondent" assigned to cover one such day of harmless warfare.

NOVEMBER 9

Birth of Elijah Lovejoy (1802) . . . Philadelphia College of Pharmacy, first of its kind, opens (1821).

A day in a monastery. A description of the long, arduous, dedicated day of a monk. Descriptions of any special activities in the monastery (for example, "Monk's Bread" is prepared at one such retreat, and enjoys great popularity in those supermarkets and groceries where it is sold to the public).

What we know about the moon. In recent years, the moon has become less of a mystery, although its hold on lovers and the writers of popular song lyrics hasn't lessened at all. A meteorologist sums up some of our new knowledge, and lists the many questions that still perplex and challenge modern science.

Cross-country in a truck. If you can go along yourself, so much the better; if not, describe the day-and-night journey from one coast to the other in a huge, powerful trailer-truck. The driver describes his route, his rest stops, courtesies of the road, safety precautions, favorite diners (is truck-stop coffee *really* so good?), speed traps, transferring loads, and so on.

NOVEMBER 10

U. S. Marine Corps authorized (1775) . . .
Stanley discovers Livingstone (1871).

Mulches. Black plastic mulches and rock mulches for winter cover—these are two relatively recent innovations that are available commercially. A landscape specialist or master gardener discusses the importance of mulches, the pro's and con's of the homemade variety, when and how to use.

A private "guide" in the museum. Many museums have now installed communications systems for visitors—who carry earphones, simply "plug in" at a particular display or master work, and hear a complete description of artist, work, or exhibit. Who donated the system; how it works; who wrote and "announced" the text; a sample of the sort of information one hears.

How to organize a nursery school. All across the country, because of the shortages (or expense) of nurseries and kindergartens, parents are organizing their own play groups for toddlers. Interview the founders of such a co-op nursery, and pass along to your readers the benefit of their experience—site, equipment, ideal number of children and parents to attend them, costs, and so on.

NOVEMBER 11

Veterans' Day . . . Pilgrims sign the May-flower *Compact (1620) . . . Compulsory school law enacted in Massachusetts (1647) . . . World War I ends (1918).*

Plan now for an outdoor room. Atriums, sun decks, peristyles—these are just a few of the forms an "outdoor room" for next spring and summer can take. Photos and diagrams of some new outdoor rooms, built locally; how to do the work yourself; expenses; using foliage for dividers.

Parcel post. We're approaching Christmas parcel time—and it's not too soon to discuss hints for wrapping; maximum sizes of parcels; ways to insure contents; length of time needed to deliver to various parts of the country; objects that should not be posted.

The Parents and Teachers Association. On a local, municipal, and state level—as well as nationally—this group is a force for educational development. Sample some of the problems being attacked at various levels right now by PTA groups—in one school, one city, one state. The successes achieved in recent months, goals for the immediate future.

NOVEMBER 12

Elizabeth Cady Stanton Day (she was born on this day in 1815).

How to get a passport. Over the years the process has been simplified and expedited—but you still have to prove citizenship, and get one of those notorious photos. How and where to apply; "rush season" at the bureau; restrictions on travel in force today.

New uniforms, new insignia, new stripes! Since World War II, there's been a change in the official dress of all the services—from colors to chevrons. A survey of these new uniforms and accessories, illustrated with photos. The minimum gear for officers and enlisted men. Style and design for service women.

Explaining the electrocardiogram. Just what do those wavering lines tell the physician? A discussion of this life-saving examination, and how it works; a comparison of a normal EKG and one that reveals heart damage; the recommended frequency for heart examinations.

NOVEMBER 13

Birth of Edwin Booth (1833) and Robert Louis Stevenson (1850) . . . Holland Tunnel opens for traffic between New York and New Jersey (1923).

Buying a second-hand piano. A piano tuner tells what to look for when you are considering the purchase of a used piano, listing the various tests and criteria he employs when called in to advise. Can the ordinary person do this himself, or should he seek the advice of an expert. (And if so, what are the costs?) Problems in moving a piano; where the piano should *not* be placed.

Legal eavesdropping. What are the rules in your state on tapping of wires and installation of various "snooper" devices? Is evidence accepted if obtained by these methods? How do law-enforcement officials obtain clearance for installation and use of equipment? Recent cases in state and federal courts.

Now it comes in a plastic bag! At the five-and-dime you can buy goldfish that come in a plastic bag; wet grain is stored in these containers; blood at the blood-bank is kept in them; plants are packaged in plastic; and at the supermarket, plastic bags are commonplace. A survey of this packaging trend, as described by entrepreneurs and a plastics expert.

NOVEMBER 14

Birth of Robert Fulton (1765) . . . "Nelly Bly" (Elizabeth Cochrane) begins around-the-world tour (1889) . . . Death of Booker T. Washington (1915).

Mosaics come back! The "lost arts" of Ravenna have made a comeback—mosaics are sweeping to new popularity in toys for children, as a new hobby for amateur artists; and in the decoration of tables for home and office. Interview a hobbyist, showing samples of his work. Discuss sources of supply, availability of instruction, the differences between modern and classic mosaics.

Ponies are profitable! Believe it or not, there's a big mail-order business going on in ponies (and in burros as well) as pets. From dealers in these attractive little animals, you can locate kids who are proud owners—and describe the fun and the duties of a young pony owner.

Sidewalk superintendents de luxe. Now the busy man who pauses to watch the construction of a building is provided with more than a hole through which to peer—he hears, in one case, tape-recorded explanations of what is going on; and at yet another site, the builders provide a little booklet answering typical questions.

NOVEMBER 15

Brazil celebrates "Proclamation of the Republic" Day.

Original prayers. Many ministers consider it important to write their own prayers as well as their own sermons. With Thanksgiving approaching, this would be a fine time to discuss and present some of the favorite, original "special day" prayers heard in a number of churches (local or nationally important).

Doughnuts, pretzels and pizzas. Now, from one end of the country to the other, highways are studded with pizza palaces, doughnut shops, and pretzel spetzelists. And such specialty stores are usually operated on a "franchise" basis. Describe the increasing popularity of these establishments; show how the franchise system works; the many varieties of these delights available to hungry customers.

Prison publications. Some of the newspapers and magazines issued *by* prisoners *for* prisoners are elaborate, expert publications. Some are quite specialized—e.g., a magazine for A. A.'s among the convict population. And some of the columnists are known from Alcatraz to Sing Sing. A survey of these magazines that reach a truly "captive" audience.

NOVEMBER 16

Diplomatic relations established between U. S. and Soviet (1933).

Misconceptions about the U. N. It's an unfortunate fact that many Americans know very little about the United Nations—and that, in many cases, what they "know" is wrong. Collect some of this misinformation about the Security Council, General Assembly, UNICEF, UNESCO, and so on—and then present the facts in the form of an interview with a government executive, an educator, a correspondent, or a delegate visiting your area.

Who said it? From "Boy! What a ride!" to "Don't give up the ship!", there's a vast heritage in our history of famous phrases and slogans. Present the statement—describe the circumstances—and challenge the reader to test his memory and knowledge.

Just what is Rh factor? People talk about "Rh positive" and "Rh negative"—but few of us really understand these terms and conditions, so vital when people hope to have children. A physician explains this blood classification, tells why it is significant, how it is recognized, why it is so important.

NOVEMBER 17

Suez Canal formally opened (1869) . . . Daily railroad service, Chicago to Portland, begins (1889).

Who comes to the recreation center? Youngsters in the morning, teen-agers in the afternoon, oldsters at night? What facilities for sports, hobbies, instruction? Special community functions—movies, dances, lectures, meetings. The center's budget; its paid and volunteer staff; statistics on attendance; aims for tomorrow.

Juke-box report. The music and record industries consider the juke-box the most reliable barometer of current musical taste. Reports go from the local level to such national entertainment publications as *Variety* and *Downbeat*. How is popularity of a record detected? By the speed with which it wears out? By some counting device built into machine? To whom does data go?

What kind of carpeting to buy? It would seem as if there are as many natural and man-made fibers used today in carpeting as there are in clothing. A manufacturer, dealer or a decorator can explain the special virtues of each fiber, its resistance to wear and dirt and stains, the differences in "feel" and pile, range of costs, and so on.

NOVEMBER 18

Antartica discovered by N. B. Palmer (1820) . . . Birth of William S. Gilbert (1836) . . . First Sunday comic section in newspaper published by New York World *(1894).*

Dad's salary and Junior's. Here's another way to look at inflation and our expanding economy—a comparison of what young people earn today on their first jobs and what their fathers would have earned, two decades ago, in a similar position. Your information can come from union officials, industrial personnel managers, or from "Junior" and "Dad" directly.

Strange strides in saws. Circular saws, electric handsaws, glass-toothed saws, and a saw that starts its own holes—these are just a few of the new saws available to make life easier (and more expensive, too!) for the hobbyist. A survey of saws, drills, and some of the other new "miracle" tools that are newly available on the market.

School bus driver. Sit beside the school bus driver for one morning and one afternoon trip—preferably equipped with a tape-recorder. A report on his deafening duties as chauffeur, referee, safety expert, deputy mother. His "usual" unusual problems.

NOVEMBER 19

Discovery Day in Puerto Rico . . . Birth of James Garfield (1831) . . . Lincoln's Gettysburg address (1863) . . . First colored newspaper supplement issued (by New York World, *1893).*

National Science Fair. Over 200,000 youngsters participate in the annual "science fairs"—in which awards range as high as full, four-year college scholarships. Profiles of local youngsters participating; their impressive projects; the winners.

The challenge of fresh water from salt. This story could very well evolve from the one above—for a great challenge to science today is finding a way to turn sea water into water suitable for drinking, bathing, and irrigation. A scientist discusses methods in use—their shortcomings, promising new developments, obstacles.

Second-hand clothing. In the big cities there are now fashionable outlets for originally-expensive, now second-hand furs, evening gowns, and wraps. But in almost all communities there are "thrift shops" where used clothing can be acquired—and, of course, charitable establishments that distribute old clothing to the needy at home and abroad. A survey of the "afterlife" of the clothes we discard or give away.

NOVEMBER 20

First bicycle with a rotary crank, patented by Pierre Lallemont (1866) . . . Marriage of Princess Elizabeth and Philip Mountbatten (1947).

What do we pay our public servants? From ditch-digger to Justice of the Supreme Court and President—what are the wages and salaries paid to the people employed by "the people"? Discuss recent increases in salaries; much higher incomes received by those in business and industry; salaries paid in early years of American history.

Sex offenders. A psychiatrist discusses a difficult and delicate question faced by parents—how to warn children about strangers who may be perverts, without unduly frightening these youngsters or giving them an unfortunate, lasting misconception of normal sexuality. You can use recent legislation or a recent example of a sex offense as your news peg.

Wedding customs. Contrast the weddings—preferably all within a week of each other, or all on the same day—of a specific group of couples of different faiths and nationality backgrounds. Changes in the ritual, songs and dances; various foods served; key differences in the service; words of congratulation; traditions.

NOVEMBER 21

Birth of Voltaire (1694) . . . Patent for a cigar lighter granted to M. F. Gale (1871) . . . Prohibition enacted (1918).

Time to check your air-conditioner. What should be done at the end of the long winter before this appliance is put back in use. Tips by an appliance repair expert on ways to stretch the life of other household appliances.

Aftermath of an accident. The news reports cover only a fraction of what occurs in and after an accident—since for the people involved, life will never be the same, and there is almost always an aftermath of hardship, hospitalization, legal problems, adjustments to be made. Your story starts where the headlines stopped.

Rack-jobber in a supermarket. This new kind of supplier keeps the stock of a supermarket's specialty shelves in good order—neat, well filled, abreast of changing seasons and new interests. In essence, he runs a little business of his own within the big business of the shopping center. Portrait of this man and his busy staff.

NOVEMBER 22

Patent for a steel pen granted (1809) . . . Death of Walter Reed (1902) . . . "China Clipper" leaves San Francisco, inaugurating Pacific air mail service (1935).

The delicate task of transporting glass. The glazier's real problems begin with the delivery of those vast panes of glass for storefronts, and do not end until the glass is securely installed. Show and discuss the many delicate, difficult phases of this fascinating business.

Swimming school. Now, when winter weather makes it almost impossible even to recall the joys of a dip in lake or ocean last summer, indoor pools are filled with young and old determined to "be able to reach the raft next July." Interview a swimming instructor, a pool owner or manager for discussion of students, new techniques in teaching, youngest and oldest pupils, training star swimmers, etc.

Medical laboratory. Here they go over slides, examine blood specimens, use microscopes and other devices to seek out the tell-tale signs of disease. Present a person-by-person, test-by-test picture of the operations of this essential participant in the battle against sickness.

NOVEMBER 23

Birth of Franklin Pierce (1804) . . . Coast Guard Woman's Auxiliary—the "Spars"—authorized (1942).

All about pearls. The differences between natural and "cultured" pearls—and then there are the frankly make-believe variety. A jeweler discusses pearls from all aspects—including the importance of "knotting" on necklaces, care and cleaning of jewels, the characteristics of an outstanding pearl, fabulous pearls in private and public collections, legend and lore.

All this—to raise funds! A person-by-person, job-by-job study of a volunteer drive to raise money for charitable purposes—through, for example, a fair, an art show, a dance, or a bazaar.

Pickets, parades and rallies. What are the rules in your community, city and state regarding picketing by strikers, parades for political or propaganda purposes, and rallies for political or economic ends. Often we do not realize the number of licenses, permissions, clearances and preparations necessary before we can exercise our rights of assembly or protest. We should also see, through the eyes of the appropriate officials, the importance of some such regulations.

NOVEMBER 24

Birth of Zachary Taylor (1784) . . . National Rifle Association incorporated (1871) . . . Barbed wire patented by J. F. Glidden (1874).

Planning a holiday punch-bowl. Now that we're in the entertainment season, a timely article could be built around famous punch recipes from famous restaurants—or the favorite concoctions of local, regional or national celebrities. Present lists of ingredients for various needs—some with liquor, some without—and for gatherings of various sizes.

What foreign youngsters learn about American history. From visitors from abroad, you can gradually get the information for a "new look" at our history—what, for example, an English youngster learns about the War for Independence, or the Spanish children learn about out battles with Spain, or the German pupil about World Wars I and II.

Combat cameramen and artists. Every service now trains men for the job of recording on film and paper the mass movement and the individual acts of a combat force. And these men are ready, too, to put aside camera or charcoal, and pick up and use carbine or bazooka. Interview a "combat artist," and show samples of his work.

NOVEMBER 25

Senaa Samma is first sword swallower seen in U.S. (New York, 1817) . . . Birth, Andrew Carnegie (1835).

"I want London, operator." A step-by-step story, supplied by the telephone company, explaining what happens after you tell the operator you want to place an overseas call. Routing your call; how your voice crosses the ocean; time required to complete the connection; charges for overseas telephone calls; the number of people and cities involved in handling one such call.

Do women really change their minds? Are women shoppers really as fickle as depicted—or more so? Your anonymous sources of information would include that paragon of patience, the shoe salesman; and clerks in hat stores, theatre cashiers, dress-shop sales people, a butcher, an automobile dealer, a librarian, and so on.

Cops' badges. Complete information about badges—their appearance, manufacture, and the number and variety used in a particular city and state. Are many badges lost? Stolen? Compare badges of the past with today's. Does an officer keep his badge after retirement? Do hobbyists collect badges? Badges for other services.

NOVEMBER 26

Birth of Henry Wadsworth Longfellow (1807) . . . New York's Pennsylvania Station opens (1910).

"Mister Toastmaster." Choose as your subject a widely-known speaker at luncheons and dinners. Along with the biographical data about prominent persons he has introduced, blunders that caused his face to turn red, the funniest jokes he has heard told, emphasize some such slant as: luncheon guests don't listen . . . what every speaker should know . . . don't tell jokes unless . . . calorie-counting on the luncheon circuit.

Step-by-step in the preparation of a church dinner. Present a case history of all that goes into an ordinary church dinner—from planning the courses to shopping and cooking in quantity. Accurate picture of time expended, costs, income, participants, guests, food favorites, what's done with leftovers, etc.

How an interior decorator works. Like a travel agent, the decorator doesn't charge the consumer, but is paid on a commission basis by the supplier. How the decorator fits the job to the client; finding sources of fabrics and furniture and art objects; unusual assignments; training; becoming a member of the American Institute of Decorators.

NOVEMBER 27

National 4-H Congress generally takes place on or about this date.

Premature babies. Describe the facilities at a leading hospital in your city for the care of the infant born before his time. Does your city—as many do—have a special "preemie" ambulance for babies born while Mom is out shopping or at a movie? If so, describe its dramatic mission.

How much do you pay in interest? A helpful, fascinating article can be developed simply by comparing the cost of borrowing at various institutions—banks, finance companies, pawnshops, on one's insurance. And take a look too at interest rates paid on installment purchases, and compare with the above costs.

Unusual experiences of a well cleaner. Long-lost articles that have been recovered from wells. The deepest wells in which he has worked; his training, and the methods he uses. Rescuing people and pets from wells and shafts. His suggested safety rules.

NOVEMBER 28

Death of Washington Irving (1859) . . . R. E. Byrd takes off for first flight to South Pole (1929) . . . Boston's "Coconut Grove" fire (1942).

"Consolidated high school." Many Boards of Education are merging several inadequate schools to make one superior "comprehensive" or "centralized" school of them, with sharing of (and the elimination of duplications in) library, gymnasium, transportation, laboratory facilities and teaching personnel. Show on the local level the importance of this promising new development in education.

Arrests by off-duty policemen. We constantly hear how policemen, out of uniform and off duty, spot criminals in restaurants, at terminals, or at a resort area. Describe some such exciting "breaks" in a case, with details furnished by a police official.

Troops aloft! Describe—and illustrate with photographs taken at a local base, when possible—the mighty, mammoth planes now used to transport soldiers by the hundred. Planes that carry tanks and other vast pieces of equipment. The great discipline required for speedy loading and unloading. The number of men needed to fly and service such planes. Speeds and distances these transports can attain.

NOVEMBER 29

Birth of Louisa May Alcott (1832) . . . Death of Horace Greeley (1872) . . . First Army-Navy football game (1890).

Printed circuits. A radio or television expert explains the new developments that eliminate wiring and reduce costs and bulk: circuits that are actually "printed" on plastic bases. He also covers the new transistors that have made small, portable sets possible. How these innovations both complicate and simplify the work of a repair man.

Theatre musicians at work. How does it feel to play the same music night after night at a theatre? What do the musicians do during intermissions? Do they have part-time jobs outside the theatre? Are there any musicians around today who began as accompanists to the old "silent" films of the Twenties?

Animals and their winter homes. The bears are now hibernating . . . squirrels spend more time in the hollow trunks of trees . . . butterflies can be found under the dead bark of old trees—indeed, the "apartments" of field and forest are filled for the winter. An expert in the field of wildlife describes these lairs, caves, tunnels, hideaways, and tells us what life is like for animals during the cold winter months.

NOVEMBER 30

Birth of Mark Twain (1835) and Winston Churchill (1874) . . . Impeachment proceedings begin against Samuel Chase, Supreme Court Justice (1804).

School excursions. Part of the job of the elementary school teacher is providing experiences—new sights, new understandings—to her class, through trips to factories, the post office, City Hall, and so on. You can survey the many places so visited, or accompany the third-graders on one such tour.

A mighty musical country! Some 1,200 orchestras—amateur and professional symphony orchestras—were meeting and playing when the Sixties began. And add to this the number of chamber music groups, the choral groups, the singers and soloists and amateur operatic groups—and you can show a slice of this country's musical scene.

Learning another language. Some folks do it with records, others with private teachers, some in adult-education classes, some in specialized language schools—but never before have so many grown-ups been attempting to master another language. Show the facilities in your area; interview students and "graduates" to learn the ways in which they use their new abilities for fun and profit.

DECEMBER 1

Founding of "Boy's Town" (1917) . . . Cyril Turner demonstrates skywriting above New York City (1922) . . . Locarno Pact signed (1925).

"In the doghouse." That's not as bad a situation as it used to be—many kennels are now heated in the winter, and boast such innovations as electric blankets and other automatic devices. Discuss unusual "architecture," multiple kennels, the combination of a kennel with a dog run. Show diagrams of a recommended doghouse the reader can make.

Fun with ceramics. Interview members of a group whose hobby is making ceramic articles. Find out what they make and how, what equipment they use, the size of their kilns, how to apply glazes and colors, how to bake a vase without cracking it. And discuss the costs of this fascinating and surprisingly inexpensive avocation.

A personal look at natural childbirth. Doctors and nurses will be able to give you information about exercises recommended for the mother before and after the child's birth, lessons in "breathing," and other preparatory measures. Discuss reactions of women who've had children both "naturally" and under very heavy sedation.

DECEMBER 2

Death of Hernando Cortes (1547) . . . Monroe Doctrine promulgated (1823).

White-collar crime. The pilferage of such items as stamps, stationery and small tools costs companies huge amounts each year; how do government and industry protect themselves against this? Detective services that specialize in white-collar crime; a case study of a business that was going on the rocks without knowing it because of these "minor" thefts.

How to do library research. A librarian or research specialist shows how to find everything there is in the library on a given subject. The various places in which information can be found—the Reader's Index of Periodical Literature, The New York Times index, card catalogs, Who's Who, specialized dictionaries and encyclopedias.

Winter photography. What filters and films are recommended when the sky is grey or snow is on the ground? How do you avoid glare? Particularly inviting subjects—a bobsled run, for example, or a child building a snowman, or a puppy in a snowdrift. Illustrated with the professionals' own favorites.

DECEMBER 3

Oberlin (first co-ed) College opens (1833) . . . Mary Baker Eddy dies (1910) . . . First woman Army officer (other than in medical branch) sworn into regular Army (Col. Mary Hallaran, 1948).

Christmas cribs. A lovely old Yuletide tradition that has gained new popularity is the making of a Christmas creche . . . and now you can find these reproductions of the Nativity Scene in homes, in village squares, on church grounds. Your approach might be to describe the crib made by one family, or to show photographs and to report on many.

Cider-making. Let's not permit this to become a lost art! Do your part by presenting favorite made-at-home cider recipes, so detailed that the most bumbling of us can follow them. And don't forget to add such special delights as mulled cider.

A roof of vines. Climbing plants (as you can perhaps see best when you visit the homes of George Washington and Thomas Jefferson) can do just what you want them to do. And so today they're being guided into making car-ports, garden dividers, or to provide shade. An expert gardener—for example, the manager of a nursery—can best advise on the choice of plants.

DECEMBER 4

Birth of Thomas Carlyle (1795) and Edith Cavell (1865).

The fascinating lumber business. Different kinds of wood come from all over the country: what are the origins of the white pine, mahogany, walnut in a nearby lumber yard? Trace one kind of wood back to a relatively local source and describe all the steps it goes through, from the felling of the tree to the delivery of the finished planks. Lumberyards are now catering to the "do-it-yourself" addicts, so include some of the special terms the lumber salesman uses—it's necessary to know them in order to get the sizes you really want. It will come as a surprise to some readers to discover that a "two by two" isn't really two inches by two inches!

"Man, that would be LUXURY!" What suggestions might elicit that response—a barber shop shave? Breakfast in bed? Interview as many people as possible for this amusing article.

New techniques in soundproofing. Architects and contractors can give you this information, as well as the various reasons people give for needing—or just wanting!—soundproof rooms, studios, offices.

DECEMBER 5

Phi Beta Kappa organized (1776) . . . Birth of Martin Van Buren (1782) and Walt Disney (1901) . . . Prohibition ends (1933).

"I was abroad last Christmas." A minister, someone in the diplomatic service, or several such people tell of their experiences with foreign Christmas customs. This can be expanded to cover traditions in many other countries, or the differences from state to state here (there are very few green Christmas trees in Los Angeles, and few purple ones in New York).

Period furniture—how to recognize it. A decorator discusses the various periods and the most readily recognized distinguishing marks of each, and explains how to tell antiques from reproductions.

The state movie censor. Who decides on the licensing of movies in your state? Do they often make cuts in films? What standards do they apply? What right of appeal is available to the exhibitor and distributor? How do the people concerned feel about recent Supreme Court decisions on movie licensing?

DECEMBER 6

Memorial Day in Arkansas . . . Birth of Joseph Conrad (1857) . . . Cokesbury College, first Methodist college, opens in Abingdon, Maryland (1787) . . . Death of Jefferson Davis (1889).

Christmas cookies. Illustrations showing how to make and decorate your own Christmas cookies, along with recipes from Germany, France and Italy —and, of course, for our own traditional cookies.

How much sleep do we need? A doctor talks about the changing needs for sleep at various ages, and gives his opinions on the questions we so frequently ask—for instance, can we ever really catch up on lost sleep? Aids for the insomniac—such as ear plugs, eye masks, sleep-inducing records—can be included in this piece.

"Piñatas." The charming climax to the Christmas observances of our Mexican cousins explained. Their portrayal of Mary and Joseph seeking lodging. The "piñata party," in which goodies fall from an earthen vessel hung high above people's heads. How to make your own piñata, well in time for Christmas.

DECEMBER 7

Delaware is first state to ratify Constitution (1787) . . . First performance by New York Philharmonic Orchestra (1842) . . . Birth of Willa Cather (1876) . . . Japan attacks Pearl Harbor (1941).

Service for all occasions. Now that it's the holiday season, the First Lady of your state (for example) talks about etiquette for formal and informal dinners, parties, buffets: invitations and replies, table settings, whether the plate should be removed from the right or the left, and so on.

Those "spatial relation" tests. The armed services, many corporations and groups administering college entrance examinations have fascinating problems to test ability to visualize numbers of cubes, block structure, the relationship of gears, and so on. Give samples so readers can test their own aptitudes.

College humor magazines. Do they change much over the years? What are their favorite topics? Who edits them? What do they cost? What's their average circulation? Do many have a faculty sponsor or censor—and are many banned? An interesting aspect of these magazines is that "complimentary copies" go from campus to campus and extensive copying is done—thus, "college humor" goes national.

DECEMBER 8

Birth of Eli Whitney (1765) . . . American Bird Banding Association formed (1909) . . . U. S. declares war on Japan (1941).

"I'll take it to the Supreme Court!" One of the relatively few lawyers qualified to plead cases before the federal Supreme Court tells of a case that began in the lowest court and went all the way up—how long it took, how many courts it went through, how much money was spent. He explains the procedure lawyers must go through to qualify for practice before the Supreme Court and tells what cases may and may not be pleaded before it.

Cramming for exams. How much good does it do? How do the grades of students who rely solely on cramming compare with those of other students? How much knowledge is retained? Cramming for exams is often done in groups—as much so that the students can keep each other awake as to exchange information. Possible photo feature.

They tried to beat the lie detector. Set up a group of students, lawyers, housewives, those in other professions, and have them try beating this device. (Who *can* fool the lie detector?)

DECEMBER 9

Birth of John Milton (1608) and Joel Chandler Harris (1848) . . . Christmas seals go on sale (1907).

From design to printed textile. Interview all of the people involved, explain all procedures. Illustrate by following one design from its inception to the store. The artist, the stencil, applications of color in various printings; transference to elaborate printing machinery; preliminary textile treatment.

The sad business of bankruptcy. What happens when a person or a company goes bankrupt? Interview a county clerk to find out the legal procedure. Do people or businesses often make a comeback after they've had to file for bankruptcy?

Unusual restaurants. The automats in New York, the famous "Hamburger Train" restaurant where food is brought to your place at the counter by a model train. Describe unusual décor, menus, "themes" of restaurants. Restaurants that aim for the family trade, with special gifts and menus for children. Restaurants in odd structures.

DECEMBER 10

Wyoming Day . . . Birth of Emily Dickinson (1830) . . . American Library Association incorporated (1879) . . . National Jewish Hospital for tuberculars opens in Denver—a non-sectarian institution (1899).

Winds—from breeze to hurricane. A "breeze" is actually a stronger wind than a "calm wind." A meteorologist describes the velocities that distinguish breeze, gust, blast, gale, storm, tempest, hurricane, tornado, and cyclone; and a civil defense official describes the way in which the latter few emergency situations are handled in your city, state and region.

If Santa were at the North Pole now. A look at his traditional home as we know it today. Who is there now, and what are they doing? What is it like physically? How about the weather?

Checking your odometer. Is that dial on your car telling the truth as it marks off the miles you travel? A sports car expert explains how to make sure it's not fibbing. Some facts: the driver takes his car to a "measured mile," and checks the odometer accuracy. Then he investigates the effect of tire pressure, odometer back lash, and a myriad of other details.

DECEMBER 11

Birth of Thomas Coleman du Pont (1863) . . . First yacht race across Atlantic begins (1866). . . King Edward VIII abdicates (1936).

Glider base. The basic construction of gliders . . . how they take off and land . . . what purposes they are used for, and what's learned from their flights . . . as related by a glider pilot at a base near your home. How did he become interested in this form of flight?

Help for children in trouble. The various agencies and clinics in your community (city, state) that have been set up to help children overcome, or live with, various physical, emotional and material problems. You'll range from speech and psychiatric clinics to homes that entertain children of working parents during afternoons, and to groups that give needy children Christmas toys.

A jockey's apprenticeship. It can be long—and it isn't very romantic! Describe the duties of apprentice jockeys at a large stable: currying, feeding and exercising the horses, cleaning out stables. What special diets do they follow? What rules and regulations? How long before an apprentice is allowed his chance to ride?

DECEMBER 12

Birth of John Jay (1745) . . . Washington, D.C. becomes capital (1800) . . . Birth of Gustave Flaubert (1821) . . . G. F. Grant patents the golf tee (1899).

Care of American Express, Paris. How this office holds messages and letters for months, forwards mail on request, and acts—more than any other European office of "Amexco"—as a general post office for Americans in Europe. Their general message and register book—flip through it and you'll find names of friends you haven't seen in years who are staying in the city and have left their hotel name and date of departure (sometimes their entire European itineraries!) for these "just in case" contacts.

Businesses on wheels. They're myriad—and range from the familiar but vanishing iceman and vegetable and fruit carts to "hot coffee" wagons, portable shoe stores, small carousels, small trucks ready to grind shears and knives, and travelling dress stores.

Tips on correct tips. Go to the people who know to get this information—a headwaiter, a shoe-shine boy, a barber, a messenger. Besides discussing the correct amount of tip for a manicure, checking a coat, and so forth, you can get amusing stories of the largest and smallest tips.

DECEMBER 13

New Zealand discovered (1642) . . . The "Fishhawk," first federal fish-hatching steamer, is launched (1879).

School windows say "Merry Christmas!" A photo feature of the windows children have decorated to ring in the holiday season. Their Santas, Christmas tree cut-outs, wreaths, paper Nativity scenes, snowmen. Photograph this material now for next year.

"The noise I just can't stand." Many people cringe at the sound of chalk on a blackboard—but others can't stand hearing knuckles cracked, bubble gum popping, and so forth. Interview a group, or a cross-section of people—and you'll turn up with some far-fetched pet peeves in the noise department.

The tutor's job. It's often a tough one. He may be called in at the last moment to get Junior through a course he's been failing for months, and find himself blamed when the young man doesn't pass. Who are the tutors in your community? Is this their full-time occupation? In what subjects do students require the most coaching? There should be some amusing (anonymous!) anecdotes to be found in interviews with tutors—especially those who coach elementary school children.

DECEMBER 14

Death of George Washington (1799) . . . Roald Amundsen discovers South Pole (1911).

Training the department store "Santa." Interview the personnel officer of a large department store. What instructions does "Santa" receive so he can live up to a role well fixed in the mind of every child? What is he told to answer when children ask for various gifts?

Thermometers—household, medical, industrial. The vast range of uses for thermometers—starting with the household thermometer used as an advertising giveaway and the familiar fever thermometer, and going to the extraordinarily sensitive instruments used in industry. They're vital in laboratories in many phases of the technician's work. Among other uses: in chemistry, photography, dairies, fish tanks—the kinds and the uses are myriad.

Crash! Smash! Sounds of a testing laboratory. Packages and containers, toys and tires, and hundreds of other objects go through scientific torture tests at this laboratory, where machines push, prod, poke, drop, drag, and joggle according to scientifically-determined standards. An insight into the unusual and vital work of the testing lab.

DECEMBER 15

Bill of Rights Day (last state, Virginia, ratified in 1791) . . . Chief Sitting Bull killed (1890).

No strikes, no boycotts, no lock-outs! We hear a great deal about labor-management problems, but too little, unfortunately, about the many situations (such as the one that obtains in the hat industry) where there have been no work stoppages for years. Present a picture of such a beneficial labor-management partnership.

"My favorite restaurant abroad." Diplomats, airline pilots, travelers, Navy officers, import-export specialists who must frequently be abroad—these are some of the people you'll interview to make your own world-wide list of gourmet dining-places. Your informants will supply local color and background; and letters to the restaurants can bring you sample recipes, photos, price information, and other details.

Radiologist at work. The physician who specializes in radiology performs the incredibly delicate task of using radium capsules, for example, to kill growth cells; or, working behind huge walls of glass, with water between the heavy glass sheets, he "aims" X-ray voltage of enormous power at the patient.

DECEMBER 16

Birth of Ludwig van Beethoven (1770) . . . Boston Tea Party (1773) . . . Birth of Jane Austen (1775) . . . First issue of Variety *(1905) . . . Rasputin murdered (1916).*

Spray your way to lovelier Christmas decorations! You and your children can have fun—and more beautiful decorations—if you use the special sprays to color pine cones, for example, silver and gold, to achieve "snow" effects on your windows and on the Christmas tree; to make a startling pink, silver and gold wreath; to make handsome wrappings.

A day with a process server. These are the people whose difficult (sometimes, in any event!) job it is to deliver a subpoena commanding the person so served to appear and testify in a legal proceeding. Women as well as men are employed as process servers; sometimes—and this is where the drama comes in—they are ducked as if they were lepers.

Contests for salesmen. From worldwide cruises to that familiar gold watch—that's the range of prizes offered as incentives to salesmen in "break the quota" contests. Now companies involve wives as well, so that hubby is reminded by her that the top prize of a mink coat would look mighty nice on her . . . and hubby goes out to sell more!

DECEMBER 17

Birth of John Greenleaf Whittier (1807) . . . First successful airplane flight (12 seconds) by Wright Brothers (1903).

Letters from kids to Santa. With the assistance of the postal authorities, parents, and tape-recorded interviews with youngsters, do a report on what's been asked of Santa in this year's crop of letters. Quiz the postmaster and primary-grade teachers to find out whether more or fewer letters go to St. Nick each year. What is done with these pleas for presents?

A pile-driving contractor. These companies specialize in wood, steel and concrete piles, on land and in water—making underpinnings for such various structures as docks, piers, bulkheads, vast office buildings and apartment houses. The necessary test borings and soil investigation. The powerful equipment they use, and such new materials as concrete-filled steel tubes.

Miracles of physiotherapy. Profile of the physiotherapist—who, under the direction of a physician, helps people regain the use of their muscles. He or she teaches the cerebral-palsied child to walk, enables the polio victim to attain greater independence, administers exercises to the invalid.

DECEMBER 18

Baltimore Monitor *is first newspaper to appear on a Sunday (1796) . . . Birth of Edward MacDowell (1861).*

Syndicated advertising—stock art. The little business can still benefit from the skill and experience of a large advertising agency and highly-paid commercial artists, since a number of firms specialize in selling complete campaigns to retailers, service firms, etc., on an "exclusive in your city" basis. Show samples of ads, drawings, photos available for various business needs; cover costs, special services, etc.

"What I hate about TV commercials." A survey of pet peeves. I'll tell you some of my own—the inevitable smile after a puff of that cigarette, the use of the word "only" when referring to the staggering prices of toys for kids, the inane conversations between hubby and wife about "Miracle Mud" or whatever the product may be.

Preparing for the Christmas rush. How the bus lines, railroads, and airlines have prepared for the vastly-increased passenger traffic during this holiday season. What is involved in scheduling extra vehicles and flights. Use of temporary personnel for clerical jobs. Statistics from past years.

DECEMBER 19

Georgia is first state to enact a birth registration law (1823) . . . Birth of Ty Cobb (1886).

Music boxes and Christmas. A collector or museum curator relates the role that the music box has traditionally played during the Yuletide season. Music boxes that are local family heirlooms. The great popularity of recordings of Christmas hymns as performed by music boxes several centuries old. The tiniest and the largest of these that can be seen and heard locally.

He deals in trophies. An insight into the business of loving cups, trophies, special plaques and medals. Describe catalogues sent to the local jeweler that offer trophies for every conceivable occasion—for winners of athletic events, for retiring dignitaries, for super-salesmen, or, most recently, as gags.

Hints on leather care. With the use of leathers on the increase—in cars, in home decoration, and in clothing—a timely article can be developed on cleaning, repairing, and treating such leathers. Your sources of information will be people in the leather field, decorators, and the dry-cleaning association of your state.

DECEMBER 20

Missouri levies a bachelor tax (1820) . . . Patent granted for first pneumatic tire (1892).

What's new in party favors? Noisemaker time is rapidly approaching, and naturally the people who make the horns, rattles, and bells have introduced a number of new ideas—including "exploding satellites," rockets, miniature bongo drums, and other items tied to the worlds of current events and entertainment. You'll see new developments, too, in the cartoons and gags on paper party napkins.

Actor's agent at work. His job is to keep his "stable" (as he calls it) of actors and actresses busy. Spend a day with this harried individual: describe his meetings, phone conversations, mailings. His reassurance of his clients. Arranging for publicity releases and special photographs. The agent's fee. His description of his headaches and successes.

Emergency! Dental plate repairs! The dental laboratory is ready to handle the many emergencies that beset the wearer of plates and bridges. Proceed from this unusual element of the lab's operations to the day-to-day duties—how a plate is made, matching the shades of teeth, new materials used.

DECEMBER 21

Forefathers' Day . . . Winter solstice . . . Birth of Benjamin Disraeli (1804) . . . Birth of Josef Stalin (1879) . . . First crossword puzzle to be published appears in New York World *(1913).*

Still time to learn the new dance steps! An interview with a dancing-school instructor or manager, emphasizing the fact that there's plenty of time between now and New Year's Eve to master the newest steps—or to learn the old reliable fox trot, waltz and rumba. The instructor also describes some of the newer dances, and reveals which are coming back.

They supply aprons, linens, towels, uniforms. The operations of a service that provides linens, uniforms, and such other things to restaurants, hotels, barber shops and beauty parlors, hospitals, and even to private homes. How they keep each batch separate, so that the proper uniforms are returned to the proper place. Emergencies with which they've coped.

Presenting—the specialist in "presentations." He makes unusual charts and graphs, poster displays and scrapbooks, portfolios and slide films—so that Businessman "A" can more easily sell his services to Businessman "B." Such presentations are used by advertising agencies, publications, job applicants.

DECEMBER 22

Embargo Act enacted (1807) . . . Birth of Edward Arlington Robinson (1869) . . . American Association of Public Accountants formed (1886).

Safety hints for the Christmas season. Special warnings from the heads of the fire, police and public safety departments on the unfortunate hazards of the season. Preventing Christmas tree fires; safety rules for decorations; the less obvious problems of overtiredness and overeating; cautions about certain toys for infants; electric shock hazards.

My day as a hotel bellhop. Arrange to take a job for a day in a hotel, giving the reader a new view of that jack-of-all-trades, the bellboy. His work as an assistant host, baggage handler, guide to the better restaurants and cabarets, and messenger boy. His income, through tips and salary. Your own insights into those folks the bellhop is delighted to serve, and those who prove quickly unpopular.

So you want to buy (or sell) a business! The role of a business broker in bringing together those who want to purchase and those who want to sell retail stores, factories, service establishments, and professional practices. He also represents investors who plan to serve as silent or active partners.

DECEMBER 23

Birth of Connie Mack (Cornelius McGillicuddy) in 1862.

Sharing Christmas with others. A community survey, showing how families can share the spirit of Christmas with others. Toys to the children's section of the hospital . . . inviting foreign students to one's home . . . distributing little gifts to the lonely old folks in a nursing home—these are just a few of the ways any family can add to their own joys and satisfactions while brightening the day for others.

Winter-weather driving. The director of highway safety describes the special threats of winter driving, from skids on ice to intoxicated drivers. He also covers such routine cold-weather problems as frozen locks and radiator systems, and lists the steps that must be taken to make a car winter-ready.

"Mr. Fix-it"—the man who repairs anything and everything. (One of these crackerjack artisans advertises that he can "repair everything but a broken heart.") Describe the jobs he faces right now; his collection of odds and ends, useful in his work; the most challenging job of repair he's had recently; valuable pieces he has restored. The repairs he is faced with so frequently he finds them boring.

DECEMBER 24

Birth of Kit Carson (1809) . . . First bicycle with a back-pedal brake patented (1889).

Charitable contributions and your taxes. An accountant associated with a charitable group explains tax deductions for gifts to such groups. Lists and explains what is properly deductible, including gifts of goods and securities as well as money.

Hanukkah. Christmas and this Jewish holiday usually come at the same time of the year. A rabbi describes this "festival of lights," which lasts for eight days, commemorating the dedication of a new altar to replace one that had been polluted. Describe the various ways in which this feast period is celebrated in temple and home by Jewish families.

Student employment. A look at the jobs done and income earned by students at a college or university who hold part-time positions. The range, from baby-sitter to music instructor or retail clerk. Put particular emphasis on jobs held by students during the vacation and holiday periods, including service with the post office and with delivery companies.

DECEMBER 25

Christmas Day . . . Birth of Clara Barton (1821).

Christmas Day—but they're at work! A sympathetic survey of the people who must be on the job today, while the rest of us can go to worship, exchange gifts, and hold family gatherings. Policemen, firemen, hospital staff members, transit personnel, cab drivers, and those who work in restaurants and theatres are just some of the many people for whom the 25th is also a day of hard, lonely work.

Present pay for ministers. Have preachers' salaries increased in line with those of people in other professions? Interview pastors and church treasurers. It is generally estimated that ministers put in a 75-hour to 80-hour week. What would this mean in terms of hourly pay?

Christmas in our town, hour by hour. You'll be able to use this feature next year. You start with one family when the kids awaken and rush to see what's at the foot of the tree; then to the next family, getting ready to go to church; then to another, preparing for the big family luncheon; and so on, home to home, place to place, to give a touching picture of Christmas in your community.

DECEMBER 26

Boxing Day in Britain . . . Battle of Trenton (1776) . . . First electric lights in a store installed (Philadelphia, 1878).

What to do with the Christmas cards you received. Those cards will be welcomed at hospitals, in play centers and in nurseries, where children will cut out the pictures, make collages, and get further delight from the greetings that have already delighted you and your family. A report on where you should send these cards—when and why.

My favorite recipe for turkey leftovers. Let's face it —this will be a needed report in many homes! And the recipes can range from turkey canneloni to turkey croquettes to turkey tetrazini. Get your suggestions from celebrities, their wives, outstanding chefs, government nutritionists. It would also be wise to include directions for a good soup with a turkey-stock base.

A survey of broken toys. You can build a ruefully amusing story around the casualties in the toy population just twenty-four hours after the boxes and packages were opened. The sad fate of the electric trains, plastic pull-toys, doll's clothes, and so on— and the harvest of hard work this all means for Dad!

DECEMBER 27

Birth of Louis Pasteur (1822) . . . Death of Stephen Austin (1836) . . . Anaesthesia (ether) administered in childbirth for first time (Dr. C. W. Long, 1845).

And now—the returns counter! If you're as courageous as a freelance ought to be, you'll volunteer to be at the returns counter at a department store in the first business day after Christmas. Anecdotes of the people returning items or exchanging them. Do the bromides hold up? Do the men bring back horrible ties and the women return nightgowns that are either too big or too small? Discuss the serious side of returns, from the store's viewpoint.

Goals for next year. With this year coming to a close, city, state and regional officials discuss what has been achieved and what still needs doing—in employment, welfare, education, transportation, public health, and other vital areas of public life.

What happens to the stock market at year's end. You often hear about year-end selling or buying for tax purposes; a broker explains how investors attempt to change their profit picture one way or the other in the last weeks of the year so that the tax report to Uncle Sam is more beneficial personally. Examples of how this can be managed.

DECEMBER 28

Birth of Woodrow Wilson (1856) . . . Chewing gum patented (1869) . . . Death of Theodore Dreiser (1945).

Imported clothing. Survey the stock of a department store known for the excellence of its furnishing departments for men and women. Show how many nations are represented—Italian silk suits, French gloves, English tweeds, Irish linen blouses, Spanish laces, and so on. Is the "American look" in clothes actually a tasteful combination of fashions from other lands?

"Education by machine." An educator describes the new "teaching machines" that are being used in a number of schools and colleges with remarkable results. These amazing contrivances cover a subject in step-by-step fashion, but are so arranged that they do not move on to the next topic until the student has correctly answered questions on the preceding material.

Custom coffees and teas. Interview a dealer in teas and coffees that are prepared to the taste of his customers—just the right blend of various beans from various countries, or the perfect mixture of this leaf and that. His attitude toward "instants."

DECEMBER 29

Nation's first nautical almanac published (Boston 1787) . . . Birth of Charles Goodyear (1800) and Andrew Johnson (1808) . . . First YMCA opens (Boston, 1851) . . . Birth of William L. ("Billy") Mitchell (1879).

How much news on radio and TV? Most stations broadcast the headlines, and a few programs of comment and analysis are heard and seen—but how does the ration of news broadcast and telecast compare with that found in the daily press? A survey, with comments, by a class in a local journalism school.

Trials and tribulations of a waiter. Pity the poor waiter—who sometimes waits and waits for an order, and then is rushed; who is given orders by a number of people in the party, who change their minds frequently; who is blamed for the sins of the chef as well as for his own. Discover and then pass on the peeves of the waiters and waitresses who serve us.

The most exclusive New Year's party in town. Will it be at a private club? In City Hall? At the Governor's mansion? At a society restaurant? Actually, there are probably several highly-exclusive parties that will make good copy—from guest list to repast, fashions to fun.

DECEMBER 30

Birth of Rudyard Kipling (1865) . . . American Political Science Association founded (1903).

Ready for New Year's Eve! We're not talking about the celebrators, but about the highway patrol, auto wreckers, the ambulances and hospitals—for the grim fact is that they will be suffering through one of the worst nights of the year. Make this a frankly "scare" report that is intended to discourage drunks from taking the wheel.

The news story I won't forget. A survey of reporters and editors about the news event of the past year they expect always to remember. Was it a space shot for one? A crime for another? An exclusive interview for a third? Use this as a new approach to a dependable, always-interesting report of the year's top events.

A look at YOUR year . . . By a bank executive, a physician, a minister, an educator, a psychiatrist—who talk about things all of us might well have hoped to achieve during this year. More financial stability, better health habits, greater evidence of faith in our daily activities, more knowledge, more compassion and tolerance. Has the reader achieved these? Make this a challenge and a goal to achieve.

DECEMBER 31

New Year's Eve . . . Birth of George C. Marshall (1880) . . . President Rutherford B. Hayes celebrates his silver wedding anniversary in White House (1877) . . . Ellis Island opens as immigrant receiving station (1890).

New Year's resolutions. You'll follow up on this later —but now you might survey city, state and regional "names" to learn what vows they've made for the New Year *re* diets, smoking, more vacation time, more reading, daily exercise, increased business efficiency, and so on. And in late January, when you've found that they've slipped, be gentle!

Predictions of things to come. From astrologers, gypsies, tea-leaf readers and such, cadge prophecies of what the coming several months will bring in the way of world affairs, employment, the weather pattern, and even Oscar winners. This, of course, is a story you'll want to follow up on later.

How we spent our money this year. A national look at American expenditures. For example, in one recent year we spent $254,700,000 for chewing gum, $107,450,000 for shampoos, $37,910,000 for stomach sweeteners—but we still skimp on education, pensions for oldsters, etc. What will next year bring?